T0244366

PLANT-BASED INDIA

Nourishing Recipes
Rooted in Tradition

DR. SHEIL SHUKLA

THE EXPERIMENT

NEW YORK

The Experiment, LLC | 220 East 23rd Street, Suite 600 | New York, NY 10010-4658
theexperimentpublishing.com

This book contains the opinions and ideas of its author. It is intended to provide helpful and informative material on the subjects addressed in the book. It is sold with the understanding that the author and publisher are not engaged in rendering medical, health, or any other kind of personal professional services in the book. The author and publisher specifically disclaim all responsibility for any liability, loss, or risk—personal or otherwise—that is incurred as a consequence, directly or indirectly, of the use and application of any of the contents of this book.

The Experiment's books are available at special discounts when purchased in bulk for premiums and sales promotions as well as for fund-raising or educational use. For details, contact us at info@theexperimentpublishing.com.

Library of Congress Cataloging-in-Publication Data

Names: Shukla, Sheil, author.
Title: Plant-based India : nourishing recipes rooted in tradition / Dr. Sheil Shukla.
Description: New York : The Experiment, [2022] | Includes bibliographical references and index.
Identifiers: LCCN 2021057661 (print) | LCCN 2021057662 (ebook) | ISBN 9781615198535 | ISBN 9781615198542 (ebook)
Subjects: LCSH: Vegan cooking. | Cooking, Indic. | Cooking (Natural foods) | LCGFT: Cookbooks.
Classification: LCC TX837 .S4656 2022 (print) | LCC TX837 (ebook) | DDC 641.5/6362--dc23/eng/20211231
LC record available at https://lccn.loc.gov/2021057661
LC ebook record available at https://lccn.loc.gov/2021057662

ISBN 978-1-61519-853-5
Ebook ISBN 978-1-61519-854-2

Cover and text design by Beth Bugler
Author photograph courtesy of the author

Manufactured in China

First printing June 2022
10 9 8 7 6 5 4

To bā, Chandangauri Shukla, my paternal grandmother,
for being my greatest source of inspiration for Indian
cuisine and creativity within it.

To my parents, Dr. Sanjeev and Sonal Shukla, for
providing me with the foundation to be who I am today.

CONTENTS

SHUKLA FAMILY

INTRODUCTION: WHY INDIA?

Tuesday was my favorite day of the week when I was growing up, because my brother Shawn and I would come home from school to some of our favorite foods, lovingly prepared by our mom. On Tuesdays (for no particular reason) and weekends, we'd get a break from our usual Gujarāti fare, which certainly didn't excite us as much as the non-Indian meals we imagined our friends having daily. Simple, semi-homemade, and very-Americanized meals, such as Mexican pizza, stir-fried noodles, and pasta with supermarket jarred tomato sauce were just some of the many dishes we looked forward to. Despite being vegetarian, my mom would even give into our pleas for the occasional fast-food chicken tender meal—perhaps because she had faced ridicule for her vegetarianism when she immigrated to the States. Looking back, I admire the love and care that my mom put into these meals, to go above and beyond to make us happy.

My parents immigrated to the United States in the late 1970s from Ahmedabad, a very large metropolitan city in the northwestern Indian state of Gujarāt. They eventually settled in a suburb just outside of Milwaukee, Wisconsin, where I was born and raised. Like many immigrants to the US, they brought their rich culinary traditions with them. My bā (paternal grandmother) lived with us, and through her, we were immersed in Gujarāti culture: food, language, and Hindu religious traditions. Like my parents, I spoke Gujarāti as my first language and ate the very same foods they grew up eating. On most days of the week, our table would be filled with traditional Gujarāti vegetarian foods prepared by both my mom and bā, an accomplished and creative home cook.

Despite the time and effort my mom and bā put into their cooking, Shawn and I weren't enthusiastic about their typical Gujarāti meals, which usually consisted of shāk (a spiced vegetable dish), dāl (a lentil stew), rotli (whole wheat flatbread), and bhāt (rice). While I didn't mind these foods, I often ate them parāne (begrudgingly). I can't say quite why, but we didn't care for Gujarāti food. Perhaps we had an aversion to vegetables in general or we just wanted to eat like our American friends to fit in. It wasn't until I left suburbia to pursue my undergraduate studies in molecular

Left: My bā (paternal grandmother). Right: A childhood photo of me enjoying one of my mom's "very American" desserts: a cupcake baked into an ice cream cone.

biology and graphic design in Chicago that I realized my true appreciation for home-cooked meals and my culinary heritage.

During my undergraduate years, living away from the luxury of daily home-cooked meals, I began cooking more frequently as a way of avoiding mundane dorm food. I had become vegetarian a few years before leaving for college, so my options were limited, and I had to figure out how to cook so that I could eat the foods I enjoyed. Through online videos and occasional phone calls home, I learned to re-create some of my childhood favorites. Cooking quickly became a new passion and my primary form of artistic expression. Living in Chicago also exposed me to people with diverse backgrounds, and I started to explore other cultures through food. And although I enjoyed tasting and learning about other cuisines, I began to crave the familiar Indian flavors I had once pushed away. So, I turned to my roots.

Just before I moved to Chicago for college, bā had left our home in Wisconsin to spend her final years with her daughters, my aunts, in

the bustling coastal city of Mumbai. I spent my summer breaks traveling to India for the sole purpose of spending more time with her. As I became more comfortable experimenting in the kitchen, I developed a deeper understanding of my family's rich food culture. While in India, I had the opportunity to enjoy the foods I grew up on with a fresh perspective and a new appreciation for the process and effort that went into their preparation. I watched my bā create dishes adored by all and even learned stories of her winning cooking competitions when she was younger.

As I continued my culinary journey back in Chicago, I came across a few documentary films, including *Vegucated* and *Forks over Knives*, that inspired me to reevaluate the way I was eating. After learning more about the food industry and its impact on the environment, animal welfare, and our health, I decided to become vegan in January 2015. To document my journey and share my culinary creations, I created my blog and Instagram account, Plant-Based Artist, through which I soon connected with a larger community of fellow cooks, vegans, artists, health care professionals, Indian Americans, and more. Later that year, I pursued my dream career and enrolled in medical school, where I began to embrace plant-based nutrition beyond veganism. While many medical schools in the United States don't emphasize nutrition in their curricula, I took it upon myself to learn more by attending conferences and connecting with physicians who incorporated nutrition into their medical practices. I discovered the profound impact of nutrition on the management of many chronic diseases, including hypertension (high blood pressure), heart disease, and diabetes. I went beyond the classroom to learn more about the impact of whole-food nutrition (vegetables, fruits, grains, nuts, and seeds) in conjunction with conventional medical therapies and earned a formal certification in plant-based nutrition. This exploration led me back once again to my Gujarāti roots.

The Gujarāti food I grew up on is a celebration of fresh produce, which I appreciated even more while traveling through India a few years after bā passed away. My wife, Rachel, and I traveled to three major cities—Mumbai, Ahmedabad, and Surat (which, like Ahmedabad, is also in Gujarāt)—to see our family. One of the realities known to many NRIs (Non-Resident Indians, aka Indians living abroad) is the necessity of social visits when traveling to India. Immediately upon our arrival, we were met with many appeals of "amārā ghare āvjo," which translates to "please come over to our home." The abundance of humility and generosity was touching; our family members were eager to host us if only for a few minutes of besvānu, or simply sitting together. One visit took us to a relative's home in Kosambā, a small town in Gujarāt. After sharing laughs and snacks made with the utmost care, we joined our hosts on a tour of their home. Upstairs, we were led through a small wooden doorway leading to a balcony. As I surveyed the narrow street beneath us, I saw a woman draped in a colorful sāri pushing a wooden cart that displayed the freshest selection of green beans, eggplant, corn, grapes, and tomatoes. It was here that I truly recognized the integral role of fresh produce in Gujarāti cuisine.

The farm-to-table concept of food is a daily reality in many

A visiting produce cart in Kosambā, Gujarāt

regions of India. My aunts in Mumbai often purchase their everyday fruits and vegetables from produce carts. I have memories of bā meticulously eyeing the freshest tindorā (ivy gourd, see page 87) from my aunt Shruti Foi's third-floor apartment in Mumbai. She'd select the vegetables in the morning and prepare them for lunch that very day; the meal was absolutely delicious every time.

From traveling to India numerous times and befriending Indian Americans from across India, I've come to appreciate the diversity in Indian cuisine. It's steeped in thousands of years of culture, religious tradition, and influence from other countries and communities. After all, India is home to over one billion people, with millions who have emigrated to other parts of the world. The collection of Indian and Indian-inspired dishes in this cookbook is a sampling of this incredibly nuanced cuisine. Though I grew up eating mostly Gujarāti food, my bā and mom would also make us dishes from other Indian regions, which they had learned to make after living both in India and abroad. I've seen this in many other Indian and Indian

American homes: cooking influenced by other regional Indian and global cuisines. This is why you'll find various South Indian and North Indian dishes throughout the book. I've painted with broader strokes here; my methods may not reflect what others define as traditional or authentic. For example, my Sāmbār (page 114) may appear to have a Gujarāti American touch; this certainly doesn't intend to detract from a sāmbār made by someone with South Indian ancestry.

While every recipe in this book is vegan, it's important to note that dairy plays a significant role in Hindu tradition and its food. Meat dishes, too, are especially important to many communities within India (of numerous religious traditions, not limited to Islam, Christianity, or even Hinduism), and this book certainly isn't meant to erase the culture behind them. Rather, it's intended to celebrate eating more plant-based foods for the betterment of our health, animals, and the environment while also paying homage to my own family traditions and heritage.

I don't cook Indian food every day, but it's what I know best. Indian cuisine can often be laden with fried foods and saturated fats, which

Top: Bā making theplā and muthiyā in India during my college visits to see her. Bottom: A photo of bā and me soon before she returned to spend her final years in India.

are linked to heart disease. But at its core, traditional Gujarāti cuisine is plant-centered and seasonal in nature, since the ingredients in a typical meal are based

Left: My parents at their wedding. Right: Rachel and I at our wedding (photo courtesy of DARS Photography)

on the produce that's available. There are lessons to be learned from these traditional ways of eating. Fresh, vibrant fruits and vegetables are not only delicious but also nutritionally plentiful and healthful.[1] Many of the recipes in this book are traditional, but I've developed others with my own Indian American adaptations, which celebrate the produce that's more readily available in the Midwest, where I live. In the recipes, you'll find an abundance of nutritional powerhouses: fresh vegetables, spices, legumes, and whole grains. Green leafy vegetables and beets, for instance, are extremely healthful foods, as they contain dietary nitrates, which play an important role in improving cardiovascular health.[2] My approach to cooking and developing recipes is also driven by flavor. I don't shy away from using oils and sugars when needed (in moderation), so the recipe does not compromise the flavors and cooking techniques that are so deeply rooted in tradition. I believe that moving away from ultra-

restrictive diets and calorie counting also fosters mental health. For this reason you will not see full nutritional details in my recipes. I hope this book inspires you to find your own balance in the kitchen, and to immerse yourself in the culture behind plant-based Indian cuisine.

WHY PLANT-BASED?

I majored in molecular biology in college, but I also studied graphic design, because I had been drawn to fine arts since childhood. My passion for both science and fine arts is what drew me to a career as a physician; I saw these two disciplines work in harmony in the medical field. I appreciate this even more as a physician practicing internal medicine, since treating patients isn't always an exact science. It requires finesse and nuance that only comes with experience. I find this is particularly true since, as it's often said in health care, patients don't read the medical textbooks—they often present differently than the way we're taught in the classroom. There's much more art than science involved in patient communication and education, which is imperative to being a successful physician. That's one of the things I love the most about practicing medicine.

In the ten years I've worked toward my medical career, I've been actively building my culinary one, too. I strongly believe that food, nutrition, and medicine are deeply connected and that even deeper are aspects of culture, socioeconomics, weight stigma, and even politics. How can we find a cuisine that balances all of these? I don't know if we ever will, since each component has its own complexities and challenges. But I do know that, if we recognize food as being so much more than what goes on our plates, we will be a step closer to achieving this balance. Culinary medicine is an emerging aspect of clinical practice that aims to do just that by educating people about the positive effects of healthful food preparation on public health.[3] I believe it's important to put thought and intention into the food that nourishes us. This cookbook embodies the values of culinary medicine; here I'm sharing what I've learned about plant-based nutrition over the past ten years, with approachable recipes as well as the practical aspects of incorporating lifestyle changes.

While nutrition and medicine have been closely intertwined for me, this isn't the norm for most medical students in the United States.[4] During medical training, I pursued my own nutrition education by attending conferences, creating relationships with like-minded physicians, reading peer-reviewed research, and earning a certificate in plant-based nutrition. In recent years, I've been heartened by the fact that the medical education system is starting to acknowledge and promote the role of nutrition education in medical training.

Lifestyle management—the use of lifestyle modifications like making healthful dietary changes or increasing physical activity—is routinely cited as first-line management and/ or concurrent management for many medical conditions, including high blood pressure[5] and type 2 diabetes mellitus.[6] Lifestyle medicine is a branch of medical practice that incorporates and encourages increasing physical activity, managing stress, fostering relationships, getting more sleep, reducing or eliminating substance use (i.e., tobacco and alcohol), and modifying diet.[7]

When it comes to diet and nutrition, it shouldn't be a surprise that fresh fruits and vegetables, whole grains, legumes, and spices are good for us. These foods are packed with plant protein, fiber, phytonutrients, and antioxidants. For instance, legumes (such as lentils, chickpeas, and tofu) are associated with lower risk of heart disease and even all-cause mortality.[8, 9] Certain compounds in tofu, known as isoflavones, have

A produce market near Ahmedabad, Gujarāt

been found to be associated with a lower risk of developing heart disease.[10] Even further, curcumin, the key phenol (chemical compound) in turmeric, has well-known anti-inflammatory and anticancer properties.[11] A plant-based diet prioritizes all these powerful ingredients.

But don't just take my word for it. Plant-based diets are supported by the American Diabetes Association, the American Association of Clinical Endocrinologists and the American College of Endocrinology, the Academy of Nutrition and Dietetics, and the American College of Lifestyle Medicine, just to name a few. The American Cancer Society encourages the consumption of colorful vegetables, legumes, fruits, and whole grains as part of their diet guidelines.[12] And the Academy of Nutrition and Dietetics states that appropriately planned vegan diets are more than nutritionally adequate—they're healthful for all ages.[13]

As a primary care physician, I know all too well how critical it is to manage chronic medical conditions, such as hypertension (high blood pressure), hyperlipidemia (high cholesterol), and type 2 diabetes mellitus. These conditions, if poorly controlled, can be extremely detrimental to overall health and longevity. Plant-based nutrition, before or with trials of medication, can combat this quite effectively. Because plant-based diets are higher in fiber, lower in fat, and higher in potassium than the standard American diet, they have been shown to be effective in improving high blood pressure.[14] A low-fat vegan diet has also been shown to improve blood-sugar control in diabetes.[15]

The evidence for plant-based diets is compelling, but it's important to find your own personal motivation for eating more plants. While many of my recipes are whole food and plant-based (with minimally processed ingredients), I do include small amounts of oil and sugar to retain the taste and authenticity of traditional Indian dishes. This is also the truest representation of the food I eat, although there's merit to eating a strict whole food, plant-based diet that otherwise excludes these foods. In recent years, the term *plant-based* has been used more broadly to describe some vegan foods that are not health-promoting—for example, I recently came across a package of "plant-based" sugar cookies, in which the primary ingredients consisted of a maximally processed combination of all-purpose flour, refined coconut oil, and cane sugar. When I use the term *plant-based*, I'm referring to incorporating more whole plant-based foods into your diet.

There are many reasons to eat a plant-based diet, but my primary motivation is based on veganism. Veganism is more than a diet; it's a way of living that excludes the use of animal products as much as possible to avoid exploitation of and cruelty to animals. This philosophy keeps me committed to plant-based nutrition. For others, their primary motivation might be environmental or health. But, above all, I believe every step closer to a plant-based way of eating is commendable, and a strictly 100 percent vegan diet does not need to apply to everyone. It's important that we are forgiving toward ourselves and that we give ourselves and others grace to make the choices that are best for each of us.

While this book emphasizes nutrition, it's important to incorporate other aspects of wellness into your life, too. When thinking about physical activity, a general goal should be 150 to 300 minutes per week of moderate-intensity aerobic exercise (such as brisk walking)[16] to make us feel our best and reduce the risk of chronic conditions, such as heart disease, high blood pressure, and type 2 diabetes. Mindfulness practices, such as meditation and yoga, can be excellent for stress management, and cooking can also be a meditative process. It promotes mental well-being, which keeps us healthier and helps us live longer.[17] Nonetheless, lifestyle modification isn't always a substitute for modern medicine. It's best to discuss any major lifestyle or medication changes with your physician.

There's no one-size-fits-all plan when it comes to nutrition and wellness, but I hope this book will get you started or allow you to continue along your own path to being the best, healthiest version of yourself.

IMPORTANT NUTRIENTS AND SOURCES FOR A PLANT-BASED DIET

In the table that follows, I've called out some key nutrients to be mindful of when following a plant-based diet. This is not an exhaustive list, and supplements, except for those listed below, are not typically necessary when a person is following a varied plant-based diet. At the end of the book, I've provided additional references and further reading if you're interested in delving deeper. For further questions or concerns, talk to your primary care physician.

NUTRIENT	IMPORTANCE	SOURCES	RECIPES AND ADDITIONAL DETAILS
Protein	Fundamental building block for the growth and maintenance of DNA and cells, immune health	Legumes (lentils, chickpeas), nuts, seeds, soy products, whole grains	Chhole (page 94), Hearty Masālā Khichadi (page 146), Mattar Tofu (page 90)
Omega-3 fatty acids	Brain health	Chia seeds, flaxseeds, hemp seeds, walnuts, supplements (algae source)	Gājjar No Halvo Baked Oatmeal (page 174)
Iron	Essential for blood production	Beans, dark green leafy vegetables, whole grains	Kale and Broccoli Pudlā (page 40), Rājmā (page 97)
Iodine	Thyroid health	Iodized salt, supplements	
Calcium	Bone health	Calcium-set tofu, fortified plant-based milks, greens, spinach	Pālak Tofu (page 101), Sunflower Sāg with Black-Eyed Peas and Corn (page 102)
Vitamin D	Bone health	Fortified plant-based milks, sunlight	Supplements are generally recommended, particularly where sunlight is not very plentiful.
Vitamin B12	Red blood cell formation, nervous system health	Fortified foods (nutritional yeast and plant-based milks)	Fortified foods, such as nutritional yeast and plant-based milks, are not fully reliable sources, so supplements are highly recommended.

INDIAN PANTRY

It's simply incredible that over centuries we've found culinary and medicinal uses for pretty much every component of thousands of plants. Here, I've listed the most important ingredients in my Indian pantry—everything you need for the recipes in this book. I've taken some liberties with these classifications for ease of understanding, so the botanical details of some foods may not be fully precise.

ENGLISH TERM	GUJARĀTI AND/OR HINDI TERMS	FORMS USED IN THIS BOOK	FLAVOR PROFILE	DETAILS
SPICES: SEEDS, ROOTS, BARK, FLOWERS, FRUIT				
Alliums: onions and garlic	Kāndā/ dungali, pyāz, lasan, lehsun	Fresh	Pungent when raw, sweet and aromatic when cooked	Use in their fresh forms in the recipes in this book to make much more delicious food.
Asafetida	Hing	Powder	Oniony, garlicky	Made from tree sap, this punchy spice is best stored in a tightly sealed container since its aroma can otherwise overtake your spice cabinet.
Black peppercorns	Mari, kāli mirch	Whole, freshly cracked	Spicy, warm	Appears less often in this book than you may expect, but when it's in a recipe, it's essential.
Cardamom	Elchi, elāichi	Whole green pods, whole black pods	Minty, floral, smoky (black)	Green cardamom has a flavor profile that is suitable in sweet and savory preparations. Black cardamom, because of the way it's processed, adds a pungent smokiness and is best reserved for savory applications.
Carom	Ajmo, ajwain	Seeds	Cooling, grassy	A little goes a long way. It cools the tongue and has an oregano- or thyme-like aroma.
Cinnamon	Taj, dālchini	Sticks, ground	Sweet, woody	A fundamental spice in garam masālā (see page 232) but be wary not to overdo it, as too much can overpower other spices. *Cinnamomum verum* (true cinnamon) and cassia cinnamon are botanically different but may be used interchangeably in these recipes.
Cloves	Laving, laung	Whole	Earthy, warm	Important for adding depth of flavor but can be left out of recipes if needed.
Coriander	Dhānā, dhaniā	Seeds	Citrus, grassy	An absolutely essential spice in this book, as the base flavoring that enhances other spices.
Cumin	Jeeru, jeerā	Seeds	Earthy, woody	Pairs perfectly with coriander and is usually combined with it in many traditional Indian recipes.
Fennel	Variyāli, saunf	Seeds, bulb	Cooling, licorice	One of my favorites. You may find different varieties of fennel seeds—a shorter, stubbier one and a slenderer alternative—at your local Indian grocer. They may be used interchangeably.
Fenugreek seeds	Methi	Seeds	Bitter	Adds a subtle bitterness, almost nuttiness, that is difficult to replicate with other spices.

SPICES: SEEDS, ROOTS, BARK, FLOWERS, FRUIT (CONT.)

ENGLISH TERM	GUJARĀTI AND/OR HINDI TERMS	FORMS USED IN THIS BOOK	FLAVOR PROFILE	DETAILS
Ginger	Ādu, adrak	Fresh, dried, ground	Spicy, warm	I find organic ginger more aromatic. Measuring spoon amounts of chopped ginger are more accurate for recipes than inch/cm measurements, since varying amounts have an impact on the final dish.
Mace	Jāvitri	Whole	Floral, fruity	The outer part of nutmeg that is sold dried. Very subtle and lovely flavor when combined with other spices.
Mustard	Rāi	Whole seeds: brown or black	Bitter, earthy	Punchy. Black mustard seeds are used in most of the recipes. You'll likely find smaller and larger ones at your Indian grocer. They're similar in flavor, but I prefer the smaller ones.
Nutmeg	Jāyfal	Whole	Earthy, warm	Best purchased whole and used freshly grated.
Star anise	Bādiyā	Whole	Warm, smoky	Rarely used here but can play well with others.
Turmeric	Haldar, haldi	Fresh, dried, ground	Earthy	A fundamental spice in Indian cuisine, found in most of the recipes here.

SALT

Salt	Mithu, namak			The salt used in the recipes is iodized table salt. If using Himalayan pink salt or sea salt, use a 1:1 ratio. If using kosher salt, you'll need to use more: a 1.5–2:1 ratio to the amount of salt the recipe specifies.
Black salt	Sanchal, kālā namak		Sulfurous	Essential in chāt masālā (see page 236).

OILS

Neutral oil	Tel	Sunflower, grapeseed		Use your preferred neutral oil in place of the suggested options.
Olive oil		Extra virgin		

BLACK MUSTARD SEEDS

GREEN CARDAMOM PODS

CUMIN SEEDS

CORIANDER SEEDS

CLOVES

FENUGREEK SEEDS

WHOLE SPICES (CINNAMON, NUTMEG, MACE, BLACK CARDAMOM PODS, AND STAR ANISE)

FENNEL SEEDS

ENGLISH TERM	GUJARĀTI AND/OR HINDI TERMS	FORMS USED IN THIS BOOK	FLAVOR PROFILE	DETAILS

SWEET

ENGLISH TERM	GUJARĀTI AND/OR HINDI TERMS	FORMS USED IN THIS BOOK	FLAVOR PROFILE	DETAILS
Sugar	Khānd, sākar	Cane sugar, raw cane sugar	Neutral sweetness	I recommend organic cane sugar, as conventionally processed sugar is not always vegan.
Dates	Khajur	Whole dried fruit, syrup	Caramelly	The only sweetener I would consider healthful, as it is not stripped of its fiber.
Jaggery	Gol, Gud	Chunks	Caramelly	A minimally processed sweetener made from sugarcane juice. It's sold in large chunks at Indian grocery stores. It is sometimes sold in 1-tablespoon pieces, which I prefer the most. Palm sugar (used in Thai cuisine) is a suitable substitute.
Maple syrup		Syrup	Caramelly	Always stick to 100 percent maple syrup, as others are usually made from corn syrup.

ACID

ENGLISH TERM	GUJARĀTI AND/OR HINDI TERMS	FORMS USED IN THIS BOOK	FLAVOR PROFILE	DETAILS
Citric acid	Limbu nā ful	Powder	Acidic, citrusy	Adds acidity when liquid is not desired.
Dried green mango	Āmchur	Powder	Fruity, tart	Adds acidity in spice blends such as chāt masālā (see page 236).
Kokum	Kokum	Dried fruit	Astringent, tart	Adds acidity in Gujarāti Dāl (page 113).
Lemon, lime	Limbu	Fresh juice	Citrusy, bright	Please stick to freshly squeezed.
Tamarind	Āmli, imli	Concentrate	Sweet, sour	Used to add acidity in Sāmbār (page 114).
Tomato	Tāmetā, tamātar	Fresh, paste	Bright, acidic	I often use tomato paste in gravy dishes (see pages 88 to 105), since it adds depth.

CHILI

ENGLISH TERM	GUJARĀTI AND/OR HINDI TERMS	FORMS USED IN THIS BOOK	FLAVOR PROFILE	DETAILS
Green chili	Lilu marchu, hari mirch	Fresh	Bright, fruity	In this book, green chili generally refers to Indian green chili, a slender, long chili that is slightly less spicy than a serrano and is readily available at Indian grocers. Other varieties of green chilies, such as jalapeño (usually milder) or Thai green chili (much spicier) may be used instead. Get to know which chili gives the level of heat you prefer.
Red chili	Lāl marchu, lāl mirch	Whole dried, ground	Warm, sometimes smoky	I generally call for one spicy red chili (Guntur or cayenne) and/or one that's milder (paprika or Byadgi, often sold as Kashmiri).

BLACK PEPPERCORNS

CAROM SEEDS

ENGLISH TERM	GUJARĀTI AND/OR HINDI TERMS	FORMS USED IN THIS BOOK	FLAVOR PROFILE	DETAILS
HERBS				
Basil	Tulsi	Tulsi (holy basil), Italian basil	Minty, fresh	Holy basil is often used as a garnish in prasād (Hindu religious offerings) and adds a nice flavor to dishes like sheero (see page 177).
Bay leaves	Tej pattā	Dry Indian bay leaves	Warm, cinnamon	Bay leaf here refers to dried Indian bay leaves (*Cinnamomum tamala*), but any variety may be substituted.
Cilantro	Dhānā, kothmeri, dhaniā	Fresh	Bright	Widely used throughout Indian cuisine for freshness. Can be omitted if needed.
Curry leaves, sweet neem leaves	Mitho limbdo, kari pattā	Fresh	Intensely aromatic, savory	Fresh is ideal and most fragrant; dried is not very flavorful and not recommended. Can be frozen.
Fenugreek leaves	Methi	Fresh, dried	Bitter, earthy	Bitter, though less so than fenugreek seeds.
Lemongrass	Lili chā	Fresh	Bright, cooling	A delicious addition to chāi (see page 198).
Mint	Fudino, fundinā	Fresh	Bright, fresh, cooling	Delicious in chutney; adds a brightness that pairs well with spicy dishes.

ENGLISH TERM	GUJARĀTI AND/OR HINDI TERMS	FORMS USED IN THIS BOOK	FLAVOR PROFILE	DETAILS
FLORAL				
Rose	Gulāb	Dried petals, water	Fruity	Intensely floral and very welcome in chāi (see page 197).
Saffron	Kesar	Threads/strands	Sweet, subtly earthy	A very necessary ingredient in biryāni (see page 134), both for the flavor and the vibrant yellow/orange color it gives the rice.
Screw pine water	Kewrā	Water	Grassy, sweet	Can add a pleasant nuanced floral note to biryāni (see page 134) but otherwise not frequently used in the recipes here.
Vanilla		Extract	Sweet, nuanced	Not essential in Indian dishes, but I like using it in cakes, like Cardamom Coffee Cake (page 184).

HUSKED/SPLIT RED LENTILS

KIDNEY BEANS

SPLIT MUNG BEANS

HUSKED/SPLIT BENGAL GRAM

WHOLE URAD DĀL

HUSKED/SPLIT MUNG BEANS

HUSKED/SPLIT PIGEONS PEAS

HUSKED/SPLIT URAD DĀL

WHOLE MUNG BEANS

CHICKPEAS

ENGLISH TERM	GUJARĀTI AND/OR HINDI TERMS	FORMS USED IN THIS BOOK	DETAILS

NUTS, GRAINS, SEEDS, LEGUMES, FLOURS

ENGLISH TERM	GUJARĀTI AND/OR HINDI TERMS	FORMS USED IN THIS BOOK	DETAILS
Bengal gram	Chanā	Whole, husked/split	The Indian chickpea, smaller than garbanzo beans and with a brown exterior.
Black gram	Urad	Whole, husked/split	The whole form is used to make Dāl Makhani (page 118), and the husked/split form is an important flavor and texture component in South Indian cuisine (e.g., Coconut Chutney, page 219).
Chickpeas/ garbanzo beans	Kabuli chanā	Whole, canned	See page 94.
Gram flour	Besan	Flour	Flour made from chanā (Bengal gram). It's different from chickpea (garbanzo) flour since chanā is a different chickpea variety, but these flours can be used interchangeably in the recipes here.
Kidney beans	Rājmā	Whole, canned	See page 97.
Mung beans	Mag, moong	Whole, split, husked/split	The whole form can be used to make an aromatic stew (Whole Moong Dal, page 117), and the split form is an essential component of Khichadi (page 140).
Nuts		Cashews, almonds, pistachios, peanuts	Unless otherwise specified, raw or roasted may be used. Extremely versatile; when blended, they can add a creamy richness; when chopped, they can add crunch.
Pigeon peas	Tuver, toor	Husked/split	Used to make the base of Gujarāti Dāl (page 113) and Sāmbār (page 114).
Quinoa	Quinoa	White, multicolor	See page 126.
Red lentils	Masoor	Husked/split	Can be used to make Tadkā Dāl (page 110).
Rice	Bāsmati, sonā masuri	Brown, white	See page 126.
Semolina	Ravo, sooji	Flour	Used in both savory (Zucchini Muthiyā, page 47) and sweet (Sheero with Grapes and Basil, page 177) recipes.
Sunflower seeds		Unroasted, roasted	Not inherently used in Indian cuisine. But when blended with water, can make for a great substitute for nut-based creams.
Whole wheat flour	Ghau no lot, āttā	Flour	Aka roti or chapāti flour. Can substitute a 1:1 ratio of whole wheat pastry and all-purpose flour.

MISCELLANEOUS

ENGLISH TERM	GUJARĀTI AND/OR HINDI TERMS	FORMS USED IN THIS BOOK	DETAILS
Eno fruit salt			Leavening agent. Available flavored and unflavored; use the unflavored variety in the recipes here.
Nutritional yeast			Inactive yeast; different from active dry or instant yeast. Great source of B vitamins (although be sure to read the labels, since not all brands are fortified). Offers a "cheesy" taste when used in creamy dishes.
Pāpad	Pāpad, pāpadam		A crisp snack made from urad dāl and spices. I use it with salad (Quinoa Kachumber, page 60) and alongside a bowl of Khichadi (page 140).
Sev	Sev		Crispy noodles made from gram flour. They add a great texture to chāt (see page 20).
Tofu			Great vegan alternative to paneer.

GENERAL RECIPE NOTES

INDIAN COOKING

The cooking techniques used in this book are not too different from the techniques used in many Western households. Some, such as fermenting and steaming (as with Idadā, a steamed rice and lentil snack; page 52), may be less familiar, but the recipes describe all of them in detail. Another important technique is tempering (known as vaghār in Gujarāti and tadkā or chhaunk in Hindi). Vaghār is widely used in Indian cooking. It involves blooming spices in hot oil to awaken their flavor by heating oil over medium-high heat and toasting whole spices in it. Vaghār is often used at the start of a recipe before adding ingredients such as rice (Mint Pea Rice, page 129) or vegetables (Tindorā, page 87). It can also be used to finish a dish, as in Khaman (page 48). For those strictly avoiding oil in their diet (beneficial for people with heart disease), this technique can be changed to simply toasting whole spices in a dry pan over medium to high heat for a few minutes or until they start to turn lightly brown.

RECIPE TITLES, LANGUAGE, AND PRONUNCIATION

In most cases, the recipe titles are in a combination of English, Gujarāti, and Hindi. Occasionally, another language will be included. This reflects the habit of naming dishes the way we do in our own Indian American household, by combining languages. The headnotes explain the titles in more detail when clarification is needed. When it comes to non-English words, italicizing can be a colonizing tactic used to further foreignize and exoticize these words. For this reason, I have very consciously flouted this "convention" and decided not to italicize Gujarāti, Hindi, and other non-English words. In addition, to assist with the pronunciation of the Gujarāti and Hindi words, I've added the diacritical mark "ā" to denote a long "ah" sound; "a" denotes an "uh" sound.

SPICES

Please do not be afraid of the lengthy ingredient lists. This is due to the number of spices used. This doesn't mean that the dish is more difficult to make. If you can't find all the spices at your local grocery store, you'll find them at an Indian grocer or online. My favorite online companies are Diaspora Co., Burlap and Barrel, and Spicewalla. I haven't compromised on ingredients for the sake of simplicity, because these spices are needed for the depth of flavor that they provide. Not only are spices absolutely delicious, but they are also extremely good for you. For example, curcumin, the compound in turmeric, has been shown to have powerful anti-inflammatory, antibacterial, and antioxidant properties.[18]

I invite you to experience authentic Indian flavors through spices, but no need to stress over an omitted spice here or there, as this won't make a huge difference. I've made some spices optional in many recipes; they do contribute to the nuanced flavor of the dish, but they may be omitted if it's impractical to keep them in your kitchen. To maximize flavor, use whole spices wherever possible. When ground spices are called for, I advise freshly grinding them at home in small quantities, in a spice grinder or with a mortar and pestle. Exceptions to this rule are chilies and turmeric, which can be more cumbersome to grind at home. In addition, many of the recipes rely heavily on the flavor of a good garam masālā (see page 232). I can't emphasize enough the importance of this spice blend; it offers incredible depth of flavor. There are many store-bought varieties available, so you may need to do some adjusting for the final amount, depending on brand and freshness.

ALLIUMS

Gravy-style dishes (see pages 88 to 105) give Indian cuisine its reputation for being heavily reliant on alliums (onions and garlic). However, some Hindu and Jain communities avoid them for a variety of reasons. As a result, many Gujarāti and South Indian dishes are allium-free by default, or at least may be optional, and this is reflected in the recipes in this book. Other people avoid alliums due to gastrointestinal upset (e.g., gastroesophageal reflux and inflammatory bowel syndrome). Gravy dishes and Indo-Chinese dishes, however, are reliant on these flavors, so I haven't recommended omitting them in every recipe.

If you choose to avoid onions, an equivalent amount of fennel bulb or cabbage is a great substitute. Regardless of your choice of vegetable, please be sure not to rush the process of cooking them. Time is flavor. That doesn't mean hours at the stove, but ten minutes instead of five will make a world of difference in the flavor of the final dish. Instead of garlic, try a pinch of asafetida or celery salt, or ½ teaspoon ginger–green chili paste (equal amounts of ginger and green chili very finely minced or pounded in a mortar) per garlic clove. However, when onions and especially garlic are called for in these recipes, you'll find them used generously. They are quite healthful: Regular garlic consumption is associated with protective cardiovascular effects.[19] You'll often find alliums combined with ginger,

which also has powerful anti-inflammatory properties.[20]

NIXING DAIRY

Dairy is universally used throughout Indian cuisine, but it is not compatible with a vegan lifestyle, for ethical, health, and environmental reasons.[21–24] Dairy milk is a wonderful source of nutrition for calves, but I believe most of us should leave it as such. The modern-day dairy industry is problematic, not only because of the immense amount of resources it takes to produce a single glass of cow's milk (compared to a glass of nondairy milk), but also because of the ethical issues with artificially inseminating cows over and over to keep the dairy production process going. In addition, the large amounts of ghee (clarified butter) and other dairy products in many Indian diets may even explain the prevalence of cardiovascular disease[25] among South Asians, despite all the protective spices and legumes. Nondairy milks, tofu, nuts, olive oil, and nutritional yeast can all contribute similar flavors and textures to Indian dishes that dairy otherwise provides, and the finished dish is just as delicious, if not more. Soaked and blended nuts offer a rich creaminess to gravy dishes (see pages 88 to 105), but for our nut-free friends, feel free to substitute an equal amount of sunflower seeds or hemp hearts. I also call for using nutritional yeast (a deactivated yeast discussed more on page 15), not typically used in Indian cuisine, to offer a cheesiness that dairy would otherwise provide.

STARTERS AND LIGHTER MEALS

India is a country of more than one billion inhabitants, and it aptly has a vast array of different cuisines. The starters and lighter meals in this chapter draw inspiration from regions all across the country. They are divided into four categories: North Indian, Gujarāti, South Indian, and Indo-Chinese & Indo-Western. You'll find more details in the individual recipe headnotes. It's also worth noting that the recipes are inspired by these four regions, but they do not represent the entire range of each regional cuisine as a whole.

NORTH INDIAN: Roasted Āloo Chāt, Tofu Tikkā

GUJARĀTI: Cereal No Chevdo, Green Pea Kachori Toasts, Dābeli Crostini

SOUTH INDIAN: Rice Vermicelli and Corn Upmā, Crispy Masālā Dosā Rolls

INDO-CHINESE & INDO-WESTERN: Chili Cauliflower and Tofu, Creamy Chili Pasta

Roasted Āloo Chāt

SERVES 4

Chāt literally means "to lick" in Hindi, and it refers to a tantalizing group of dishes often served street-side throughout India. Chāt can be savored anywhere and has made its way into restaurants and homes around the globe. It awes through its layers of textures and flavors (spicy, sweet, tangy, salty, bitter). This recipe uses the humble āloo (potato), one of the most popular chāt ingredients. The potatoes are often fried, but I suggest roasting them, which is easier for the home cook. Roasting ensures that the potatoes are crisp on the outside and fluffy on the inside. Use this recipe as a guide for experiencing this quintessential Indian delicacy.

PREP TIME 15 MINUTES
BAKE TIME 40 MINUTES
ASSEMBLY TIME 5 MINUTES

ROASTED POTATOES

2 russet potatoes (about 16 ounces/450 g), peeled if desired and cut into 1-inch (2.5 cm) chunks

1 teaspoon salt, plus more to taste

1 to 2 tablespoons olive oil

½ teaspoon garam masālā (see page 232)

CHĀT

2 tablespoons unsweetened plain nondairy yogurt (see page 223)

2 tablespoons Mint Cilantro Chutney (page 212)

2 tablespoons Date Chutney (page 215)

2 tablespoons sev (ideally thin or nylon), optional

2 generous pinches of chāt masālā (see page 236)

2 tablespoons chopped cilantro or mint

Other toppings, such as pomegranate arils or finely diced onion, tomatoes, bell peppers, carrots, or cucumber, as desired

1 Preheat the oven to 450°F (230°C).

2 Place the potatoes in a large pot and add enough water to cover. Add the salt. Bring to a boil, then reduce the heat to a simmer. Cook, uncovered, until fork-tender, 8 to 10 minutes. (The potatoes will finish cooking in the oven.)

3 Drain the potatoes in a colander. Place them onto a large baking sheet and toss with oil until well coated. Spread the potatoes on the baking sheet, ensuring that the pieces don't touch each other.

4 Roast the potatoes for about 40 minutes, until browned and crisp, flipping halfway through. Remove from the oven, sprinkle with garam masālā and salt to taste, and toss until the potatoes are evenly seasoned.

5 Place the potatoes onto a large serving plate. Top with the yogurt, chutneys, sev, chāt masālā, cilantro, and other toppings as desired. Serve immediately to prevent the potatoes from getting soggy.

VARIATION Other vegetables, such as cauliflower, may be used instead of potatoes. Cut 1 medium cauliflower (about 19 ounces/550 g) into bite-size florets and place them onto a large baking sheet. Toss with 1 to 2 tablespoons olive oil until well coated. Roast at 450°F (230°C) for about 40 minutes, until starting to char. Season with garam masālā and salt, and layer the other chāt ingredients as in step 5.

Tofu Tikkā

SERVES 2 TO 4

Tikkā is a northern Indian dish involving marinated protein or vegetables cooked in a tandoor, or clay oven. My version is made with marinated tofu baked on skewers in a conventional oven to mimic the traditional cooking vessel, which adds a char and smokiness to the dish. Using smoked paprika further pays tribute to the traditional cooking technique. This tikkā is best served hot with cooling Mint Cucumber Rāitā (page 224) or Mint Cilantro Chutney (page 212) and is delicious in lettuce wraps as well. For lettuce wraps, dice the tofu and vegetables into smaller pieces after cooking and fill the lettuce leaves just before serving. Note that this recipe requires an overnight marinade to maximize flavor, so be sure to plan ahead!

PREP TIME 12 TO 24 HOURS
COOK TIME 30 MINUTES

TIKKĀ

⅔ cup (160 g) unsweetened plain nondairy yogurt (see page 223)

3 tablespoons tomato paste

6 garlic cloves, grated (about 1½ tablespoons)

1 tablespoon grated ginger

2 teaspoons fresh lime juice (about ¼ lime)

2 teaspoons garam masālā (see page 232)

1 teaspoon smoked paprika

1 teaspoon salt

½ teaspoon ground turmeric

½ teaspoon ground red chili

½ teaspoon black salt

One 14-ounce (400 g) block extra-firm tofu, drained and pressed for 1 hour (see Ingredient Tip), cut into 1-inch (2.5 cm) cubes

½ medium red onion, cut into 1-inch (2.5 cm) chunks

1 to 2 bell peppers (any color), cut into 1-inch (2.5 cm) cubes

A generous pinch of chāt masālā (see page 236)

Roughly chopped cilantro or mint

Lemon or lime wedges

Mint Cucumber Rāitā (page 224) or Mint Cilantro Chutney (page 212), optional

1 In a large mixing bowl, whisk together the yogurt, tomato paste, garlic, ginger, lime juice, garam masālā, paprika, salt, turmeric, red chili, and black salt. Adjust seasoning to taste. The mixture should be pungent, spicy, and salty.

2 Add the tofu, onion, and bell pepper to the mixing bowl and stir gently until each piece is well coated. Transfer to an airtight container and refrigerate overnight, or up to 24 hours.

3 When ready to cook, preheat the oven to 450°F (230°C). Remove the mixture from the refrigerator and stir, then skewer onto 4 to 6 stainless-steel or bamboo skewers. If using bamboo skewers, they must first be soaked in water for 1 hour. Alternate the tofu, pepper, and onion on the skewers. Reserve any remaining marinade.

4 Line the bottom of a 9 x 9 x 2-inch (23 x 23 x 5 cm) square baking dish with foil (for easier cleanup). Balance the skewers on top of the baking dish rims so the tofu is touching neither the bottom of the pan nor its neighbor.

5 Bake the tofu skewers for 15 minutes, until starting to brown in spots. Remove from the oven, brush with the remaining marinade, rotate each skewer 180 degrees, then return to the oven for an additional 10 minutes, until browning in spots again. If desired, broil for a minute or two to obtain a char reminiscent of tandoor cooking.

6 Remove from the oven and sprinkle with chāt masālā to taste and chopped cilantro. Serve hot with lemon wedges and rāitā if desired.

INGREDIENT TIP Use a tofu press for best results, but if not available, you can place the tofu between two paper towels or clean kitchen towels. Place a flat plate or cutting board on top of the tofu and a few heavy cans (like beans or soup) on top of the plate.

Cereal No Chevdo

SERVES 10

Chevdo is a Gujarāti word that refers to a crunchy snack that is universal across India. Each region of India has its own version, with names like namkeen or chivdā in the north, and mixture in the south. Some versions are even named after their region of origin, such as Bombay Mix and Nadiyādi Bhusu. Many immigrants from India to the United States have developed a chevdo made from American breakfast cereals (see Tip), and this one is my mom's version. Use this as a starting point and experiment with your own favorite (non-sugary) cereals!

PREP TIME 5 MINUTES
COOK TIME 10 MINUTES

4 cups (120 g) crisp brown rice cereal

2 cups (55 g) corn flakes

1½ tablespoons extra virgin olive oil

14 fresh curry leaves

⅓ cup (50 g) unsalted raw or roasted cashews

½ teaspoon ground turmeric

¼ to ½ teaspoon ground red chili

3 tablespoons golden raisins

½ teaspoon cane sugar

¼ teaspoon citric acid, ground to a powder, optional

Salt, to taste

1 Combine the cereals in a large mixing bowl and set aside.

2 Heat the oil in a large pot over medium-high heat until shimmering, about 30 seconds. Add the curry leaves and stir until crisp, about 30 seconds. Add the cashews and stir until toasted, 2 to 3 minutes. Add the turmeric, red chili, and raisins, and stir until well combined, about 30 seconds.

3 Reduce the heat to medium-low, then add the cereal, sugar, citric acid (if using), and salt to the pot. Stir continuously, until the cereal is lightly toasted and evenly coated with the oil and spices, 3 to 4 minutes.

4 Remove the pot from the heat and allow to cool completely. Transfer the chevdo to an airtight container and enjoy within 2 weeks.

TIP Brand name cereals may not be vegan, but there are organic and vegan versions of the two cereals used in this recipe, so make sure to check the package to confirm.

Green Pea Kachori Toasts

SERVES 2 TO 4

I've drawn inspiration for these toasts from a popular Gujarāti snack called lilvā kachori, which consists of a sweet and spicy fresh lilvā (pigeon pea) filling encased in crisp, bite-size pastry. The original version is quite labor-intensive since it involves making individual kachori one at a time. To simplify the process, I developed a similar filling made from green peas and paired it with toast.

PREP TIME 5 MINUTES
COOK TIME 10 MINUTES

GREEN PEA TOPPING

1 teaspoon coriander seeds

½ teaspoon cumin seeds

½ teaspoon fennel seeds

1 teaspoon extra virgin olive oil

1 teaspoon grated ginger

1 green chili, seeded and minced, or to taste

1½ cups (200 g) frozen peas, thawed

1 tablespoon golden raisins, roughly chopped

6 unsalted cashews, roughly chopped

Salt, to taste

TOASTS

4 slices seeded whole grain bread or preferred bread

1 ripe avocado

Lime juice, to taste

Salt, to taste

Freshly chopped cilantro or mint, optional

Microgreens, optional

1 Gently crush the coriander, cumin, and fennel seeds in a mortar or grind roughly in a spice grinder.

2 Heat the oil in a sauté pan over medium heat. Add the crushed seeds and toast until fragrant, about 30 seconds. Add the ginger and chili and stir for a few seconds longer.

3 Add the peas and sauté until tender, 3 to 4 minutes. Season with salt. Add the raisins and cashews, stir well, and remove from the heat.

4 Add the pea mixture to a food processor and pulse until roughly blended (or mash with a fork). Adjust salt to taste and set aside.

5 Toast the bread slices. Meanwhile, mash the avocado with lime juice and salt to taste. Spread a layer of mashed avocado onto each toast and top with a quarter of the pea mixture. Repeat with the remaining 3 toasts.

6 Garnish the toasts with freshly chopped cilantro and microgreens, if desired, and serve immediately.

Dābeli Crostini

MAKES 14 TO 16 CROSTINI

The inspiration for this perfect party appetizer comes from dābeli (which means "pressed" in Gujarāti), a pressed sandwich originating from Kutch, Gujarāt, the land of my maternal grandparents. The sandwiches are filled with a spiced potato mixture and served with toppings reminiscent of chāt (see page 20). I didn't gain full appreciation for dābeli until I traveled to Kutch in college. Here, I chose to pair these flavors with crostini. Making these crostini always takes me back in all the best ways. The ingredients may not make sense at first, but the flavors come together perfectly.

PREP TIME 10 MINUTES
COOK TIME 30 MINUTES

POTATO TOPPING

1 russet potato (about 240 g), peeled and cut into ¾-inch (2 cm) cubes

½ teaspoon salt, plus more as needed

1½ teaspoons white sesame seeds

½ teaspoon coriander seeds

½ teaspoon cumin seeds

½ teaspoon fennel seeds

1 teaspoon garam masālā (see page 232)

1 teaspoon lime juice (about ¼ lime), or to taste

½ to 1 teaspoon ground mild red chili

¼ teaspoon black salt

CROSTINI

1 demi-baguette, cut into ½-inch (13 mm) slices

1 tablespoon extra virgin olive oil

1 garlic clove

2 tablespoons date syrup

1 teaspoon fresh lime juice

¾ teaspoon chāt masālā (see page 236)

2 tablespoon roasted peanuts

1 tablespoon pomegranate arils, optional

1 tablespoon unsweetened coconut, freshly grated or thawed

1 tablespoon sev (thin or nylon)

1 tablespoon chopped cilantro

1 Preheat the oven to 400°F (200°C).

2 To prepare the potato topping, place the chopped potato in a saucepan and cover with enough water to submerge them; stir in about ½ teaspoon salt and bring to a boil. Reduce the heat to a simmer and cook for about 15 minutes or until fully tender. Drain the water, transfer the potato to a large bowl, and mash with a potato masher, ricer, or fork.

3 While the potato is cooking, combine the sesame seeds, coriander seeds, cumin seeds, and fennel seeds, and toast in a dry pan over medium heat until fragrant and starting to brown, about 5 minutes. Transfer to a mortar or spice grinder and grind until powdery. Mix together the spice blend and cooked potatoes, then add the garam masālā, lime juice, chili, and black salt. Taste and adjust the seasoning.

4 To prepare the crostini, lay the bread slices onto a baking sheet and brush each one evenly with oil. Bake for about 8 minutes, until crisp and golden. Remove from the oven and rub each piece with the garlic clove.

5 Place 1 heaped tablespoon of potato topping onto each crostino, pressing and spreading evenly with a spoon. Place the crostini onto a serving plate.

6 To serve, whisk together the date syrup, lime juice, and chāt masālā and drizzle the mixture evenly over the crostini.

7 Sprinkle the peanuts, pomegranate (if using), coconut, sev, and cilantro over the crostini and serve immediately.

Rice Vermicelli and Corn Upmā

SERVES 4 TO 6

This recipe brings back memories of a dish my bā (paternal grandmother) made frequently for breakfast or a snack. Vermicelli upmā itself is a common South Indian dish made from thin rice or semolina noodles. My bā's spin on it always included corn, which is the perfect addition to these pleasantly tangy and nutty noodles. You can also add other veggies, such as carrots and peas, if you wish.

PREP TIME 15 MINUTES
COOK TIME 10 MINUTES

8 ounces (225 g) rice vermicelli (see Note)

2 tablespoons neutral oil, such as sunflower

1½ tablespoons split white urad dāl

2 teaspoons black mustard seeds

¼ teaspoon asafetida

14 fresh curry leaves, torn, optional but recommended

1 green chili, minced

1½ cups (200 g) fresh or frozen corn kernels

½ teaspoon ground turmeric

1 teaspoon salt or to taste

2 to 3 tablespoons fresh lime juice (about 1 lime)

3 tablespoons roughly chopped cilantro

¼ to ½ cup (35 to 70 g) roughly chopped roasted cashews or peanuts, optional

Lime wedges

1 Soak the noodles in plenty of hot water until softened, 10 to 15 minutes. Drain the noodles and roughly chop them with a knife or kitchen shears. Set aside.

2 Heat the oil in a wok or large saucepan over medium-high heat. Add the urad dāl and heat until fragrant and just starting to turn light brown, about 1 minute. Add the mustard seeds and asafetida, and heat until the seeds crackle, about 30 seconds. Reduce the heat to medium, add the curry leaves (if using) and chili, and cook for 30 seconds. Cover to reduce the spattering.

3 Add the corn and cook for 3 to 4 minutes, stirring frequently. Add the noodles, turmeric, and salt, and stir until all the ingredients are fully combined, 1 to 2 minutes. Remove from the heat, then add the lime juice and additional salt, if needed. Toss in the cilantro and cashews (if using) and serve with lime wedges.

NOTE At Indian stores, rice vermicelli may be sold as broken pieces in a bag; these may also be used.

Crispy Masālā Dosā Rolls

SERVES 8

Crisp paper masālā dosā, consisting of a thin rice-and-lentil exterior and a spiced potato filling, is a crown jewel of South Indian cuisine. I was inspired by the flavors and textures of this classic dish to create this appetizer, which is always a crowd favorite in our home. Traditional dosā are made individually on the stovetop, making it difficult to have multiple dosā ready so people can eat together. While this version requires a bit of advance prep, everyone can enjoy the piping hot, crispy rolls at once. Note that these rolls contain ingredients not typically found in masālā dosā (i.e., carrots, sesame seeds), but I've included them for added flavor and texture. This dish is best served with Coconut Chutney (page 219) or Sāmbār (page 114). Be sure to thaw the frozen phyllo in the refrigerator overnight. I like to make the filling the night before as well.

PREP TIME 1 HOUR
BAKE TIME 1 HOUR

FILLING

1 pound (454 g) red potatoes

1 teaspoon salt, plus more to taste

1 tablespoon neutral oil, such as sunflower

2 teaspoons split white urad dāl

1½ teaspoons black mustard seeds

10 fresh curry leaves, torn

¼ teaspoon asafetida, optional

1 red onion, diced (about 2 cups/ 300 g)

1 green chili, seeded, if desired, and minced

2 teaspoons grated ginger

2 carrots, grated (about ¾ cup/75 g)

2 teaspoons ground coriander

1 teaspoon ground cumin

½ teaspoon ground turmeric

1 teaspoon lime juice, or to taste

ROLLS

1-pound (454 g) package frozen phyllo (about eighteen 13 x 18-inch/33 x 46 cm sheets), thawed

Neutral oil or cooking spray, as needed

1 tablespoon white sesame seeds, optional

Coconut Chutney (page 219) or Sāmbār (page 114), optional

1 Place the potatoes in a saucepan; add 1 teaspoon salt and cover with cold water. Bring to a boil, reduce the heat to a simmer, and cook until fork-tender, about 15 minutes.

2 Drain and transfer the potatoes to a large mixing bowl. Mash the potatoes and set aside.

3 Heat the oil in a large pan over medium-high heat. Add the urad dāl and heat until it starts to turn light brown, about 30 seconds, then add the mustard seeds and heat until they start to pop, about 30 seconds.

4 Reduce the heat to medium, add the curry leaves and asafetida (if using), and stir for a few seconds. Add the onion and a pinch of salt, and continue to cook until softened and starting to brown, about 10 minutes.

5 Add the green chili and ginger and stir until fragrant, about 1 minute. Add the carrots and continue to cook until tender, about 3 minutes more.

6 Stir in the coriander, cumin, and turmeric, and remove from heat. Mix in the lime juice and adjust the salt to taste. Allow the filling to cool completely (see Prep Tip).

7 When ready to assemble and bake, preheat the oven to 375°F (190°C).

8 Divide the filling into 6 equal portions (about 5 to 6 tablespoons per portion).

9 Prepare the rolls by rolling out the stack of phyllo sheets, keeping them covered with a damp kitchen towel to prevent drying. Working quickly, transfer one sheet onto a clean work surface and spray or brush a thin layer of oil evenly over it. Layer a second sheet of dough and oil again. Repeat again with the third sheet.

10 Lay an even "log" of filling along the shorter end of the phyllo, about 1 inch (2.5 cm) from the end. Roll tightly and place into a greased 9 x 13-inch (22 x 23 cm) baking dish. Brush the top with a bit more oil to keep from drying and keep covered with a kitchen towel. Continue making rolls as in step 9 until you have 6 rolls. Place them side by side in the baking dish and sprinkle with sesame seeds (if using).

11 Bake on the upper rack of the oven for 45 to 55 minutes, until the top is evenly golden brown and crisp. Allow to cool for about 5 minutes, cut into desired lengths with a sharp knife, and serve immediately with coconut chutney, if desired. The rolls will stay crisp for about 1 hour but may become soggy eventually (see Storage Tip).

PREP TIP The filling can be made ahead; transfer to an airtight container and refrigerate for up to 24 hours, if desired.

STORAGE TIP Leftovers may be stored in the refrigerator and reheated in an oven at 375°F (190°C) for 10 to 15 minutes, until crisp.

Chili Cauliflower and Tofu

SERVES 4

There's no question that Indo-Chinese cuisine is adored across India and abroad for its tangy, salty, and spicy flavors. This dish of cauliflower and tofu (both sponges for all things flavorful) has classic Indo-Chinese flavors, primarily umami and spicy. Roast both before stir-frying to enhance and develop their textures.

PREP TIME 1 HOUR
COOK TIME 1 HOUR

TOFU

1 tablespoon cornstarch

1 tablespoon neutral oil, such as sunflower

1 tablespoon low-sodium soy sauce (or tamari, if gluten-free)

One 14-ounce (400 g) block extra-firm tofu, drained and pressed for 1 hour and cut into ¾-inch (2 cm) cubes

CAULIFLOWER

1 medium cauliflower (about 19 ounces/ 550 g) cut into bite-size florets

1½ teaspoons neutral oil, such as sunflower

Pinch of salt

SAUCE

2 tablespoons low-sodium soy sauce (or tamari)

2 tablespoons maple syrup or desired sweetener

1 tablespoon tomato paste

1 tablespoon rice vinegar

1 tablespoon sriracha or sambal oelek, to taste

2 teaspoons cornstarch

¼ teaspoon freshly cracked black pepper

STIR-FRY

1 tablespoon neutral oil, such as sunflower

2 teaspoons grated ginger

6 garlic cloves, minced (about 1½ tablespoons)

4 to 6 scallions, sliced, white and green parts separated

3 dried red chilies, optional

Salt, to taste

Jasmine rice (or preferred alternative), optional

1 Preheat the oven to 425°F (220°C). Line two large baking sheets with parchment paper.

2 To prepare the tofu, whisk together the cornstarch, oil, and soy sauce in a large bowl. Add the tofu and mix gently with a spatula until each piece is coated. Place the tofu onto one baking sheet in an even layer, ensuring that the pieces are not touching.

3 To prepare the cauliflower, place the florets onto the other baking sheet. Drizzle with oil and sprinkle with salt. Massage the oil in the florets until each piece is coated, then spread the pieces into a single layer, ensuring that the pieces are not touching.

4 Place the tofu sheet in the oven on the middle rack and the cauliflower sheet on the top rack. Bake for 20 minutes, then flip the tofu and cauliflower pieces to evenly roast both sides. Return to the oven and bake for about 20 minutes, until the cauliflower is tender and charred and the tofu is firm, crisp, and lightly charred. Remove from the oven and keep near the stove.

5 While the tofu and cauliflower are baking, whisk together the soy sauce, maple syrup, tomato paste, vinegar, sriracha, cornstarch, and pepper in a small bowl with ½ cup (120 ml) water until well incorporated. Leave the bowl near the stove.

6 Heat a large wok or sauté pan over medium-high heat. Add the oil and heat until it shimmers and easily coats the pan. Add the ginger, garlic, white part of the scallions, and red chilies (if using), and cook until lightly browned, 1 to 2 minutes.

7 Add the reserved sauce and simmer until bubbly and starting to thicken, about 1 minute.

8 Add the tofu and cauliflower and stir to coat. Simmer, stirring occasionally, until the sauce thickens, 2 to 3 minutes. Taste and adjust for salt.

9 Garnish with the green part of the scallions and serve hot with rice, if desired.

VARIATION For an allium-free variation, substitute sambal oelek for the sriracha, omit the garlic and scallion, and use 1 additional teaspoon grated ginger.

Creamy Chili Pasta

SERVES 2 TO 4

Growing up in the United States in the 1990s, I often ate macaroni and cheese (boxed, of course) when I came home hungry after school. In college I started experimenting with Indian flavors and began to make my own version from scratch. I've since veganized it, and while completely dairy-free, it's just as creamy and satisfying as the original. I like to pair it with roasted broccoli.

PREP TIME 10 MINUTES
COOK TIME 30 MINUTES

SAUCE

1 russet potato (about 240 g), peeled and chopped into 1-inch (2.5 cm) chunks

1 carrot (about 80 g), cut into 1-inch (2.5 cm) pieces

⅓ cup (50 g) unsalted cashews, raw or roasted

⅓ cup (50 g) diced roasted red pepper, jarred or freshly roasted

1 cup (240 ml) low-sodium vegetable broth, plus more as needed

3 tablespoons nutritional yeast (see Note 1)

1 tablespoon fresh lemon juice (about ½ lemon)

¾ teaspoon salt

¼ teaspoon smoked paprika (see Note 2)

¼ teaspoon freshly cracked black pepper

PASTA

8 ounces (227 g) whole wheat pasta, such as farfalle or penne, or desired variety

Salt, to taste

½ tablespoon extra virgin olive oil

2 garlic cloves, minced, optional

1 jalapeño pepper, minced (see Note 3)

½ teaspoon toasted and ground cumin and/or garam masālā (see page 232), optional

Freshly chopped cilantro or parsley, optional

Roasted broccoli (see Note 4)

1 Place the potato, carrot, cashews, and red pepper in a large saucepan and add water to cover. Bring to a boil, reduce the heat to a simmer, and cook until the vegetables are tender and falling apart, about 15 minutes. Drain and add the ingredients to a blender.

2 Add the broth, nutritional yeast, lemon juice, salt, paprika, and black pepper to the blender and blend on high until smooth and creamy.

3 Cook the pasta in generously salted water according to package instructions.

4 Once the pasta is about halfway cooked, heat a large pan over medium heat. Add the oil, garlic, and jalapeño, and cook until lightly browned, about 2 minutes. Add the sauce and mix until bubbling, 2 to 3 minutes. Reduce the heat to low.

5 When the pasta is done, drain and add it to the pan with the sauce (see Note 5). Stir to coat and continue to heat until incorporated. Adjust the salt to taste and add cumin or garam masālā, if desired, for an added Indian touch.

6 Serve warm, garnished with freshly chopped cilantro or parsley, if desired, and with the roasted broccoli.

NOTES

1 Nutritional yeast is used often in vegan recipes to mimic a "cheesy" taste. This ingredient is very different from active dry or rapid rise yeast, which cannot be used as a substitute; feel free to omit entirely if unavailable.

2 Smoked paprika gives this dish a mild smoky flavor. Substitute ground mild red chili or sweet paprika for a non-smoky option.

3 The jalapeño adds heat and additional flavor to this dish. Seed or choose any other variety of chili to your taste and desired heat level.

4 To roast broccoli, cut a head into florets, toss with a bit of olive oil, salt, and pepper, and roast at 400°F (200°C) for about 20 minutes, until tender and starting to char. Toss with lemon zest after cooking, if desired.

5 There's no need to reserve any pasta water as you may do when making other pasta dishes. The sauce is already quite starchy, so if additional liquid is needed, use water or more vegetable broth.

FARSĀN

Snacks
and Sides

Farsān are savory snacks, enjoyed throughout the day, that are a hallmark of Gujarāti cuisine. The dishes in this chapter can be enjoyed as an appetizer or snack, with a cup of Masālā Chāi (page 197), as a savory breakfast, or alongside a thāli meal, which consists of virtually any combination of vegetable dish (see pages 66 to 87), dāl (see pages 106 to 123), rice (see pages 124 to 149), and rotli (see pages 150 to 165). Some of these dishes require advance prep, so they're perfect for enjoying on a weekend or for serving to special guests. You'll find classic Gujarāti favorites, such as Khaman (page 48), savory steamed cakes that have an addictive taste and texture.

Kale and Broccoli Pudlā

SERVES 2 TO 4

Think of pudlā, also known as cheelā, as a cross between a pancake and a crêpe. They're naturally gluten-free, as they are made from besan (Bengal gram flour, see page 15). I like to add kale and broccoli to pudlā to give them a deep green color and the fiber, iron, calcium, and other wonderful nutrients that accompany it. Serve them with green chutney (see page 212). They can also be a gluten-free alternative to Rotli (page 155).

PREP TIME 10 MINUTES
COOK TIME 25 MINUTES

1 cup (55 g) packed, roughly chopped baby kale or spinach

1 cup (80 g) finely chopped broccoli

1 cup (115 g) besan or chickpea flour

2 garlic cloves, optional

1 teaspoon minced ginger

1 teaspoon cumin seeds

½ teaspoon baking powder

¼ teaspoon ground red chili

¼ teaspoon ground turmeric

½ teaspoon salt, or to taste

Olive oil or cooking spray, as needed

Freshly chopped cilantro or mint

Green chutney (see page 212)

1   Place the kale, broccoli, besan, garlic (if using), ginger, cumin, baking powder, chili, turmeric, and salt in a blender with 1 cup (240 ml) water. Blend to form a thin batter. The broccoli can also be stirred in after blending, to retain some of its texture.

2   Heat a nonstick pan over medium heat. Brush or spray a thin layer of oil in the pan and pour in ¼ cup (60 ml) batter. Spread the batter in a circular motion using a metal spoon, beginning in the center and moving outward. Heat until it begins to appear dry on top, about 2 minutes.

3   Flip over and continue cooking until lightly browned, 2 minutes longer. Repeat with the remaining batter. Garnish with cilantro and serve with green chutney.

Makāi No Chevdo

SERVES 2 TO 4

The term chevdo typically refers to a crunchy snack (as in Cereal No Chevdo, page 24), but makāi no chevdo is essentially Gujarāt's take on creamed corn. I firmly believe that every season needs something cozy, and this is one to enjoy during corn's favorite season: summer! Since corn maintains much of its glory when frozen, this dish is a welcome addition to the table any time of the year.

PREP TIME 20 MINUTES
COOK TIME 15 MINUTES

3 cups (400 g) corn kernels
  (fresh from 2 ears or frozen and
  thawed)

¼ cup (35 g) unsalted cashews,
  raw or roasted, soaked in ½ cup
  (120 ml) hot water for 15 minutes

1 tablespoon extra virgin olive oil

1 small cinnamon stick
  (1 to 2 inches/2.5 to 5 cm)

½ teaspoon black mustard seeds

Pinch of asafetida, optional

2 garlic cloves, grated, optional

1 teaspoon grated ginger

½ green chili, seeded if desired,
  minced

8 fresh curry leaves, torn, optional
  but recommended

¼ teaspoon ground coriander

¼ teaspoon ground cumin

¼ teaspoon ground turmeric

¼ teaspoon salt, plus more to taste

2 to 3 teaspoons lime juice
  (about ½ lime), or to taste

Freshly chopped cilantro, optional

Sev (thin or nylon), optional

1   Put the corn kernels into a blender or food processor and blend until broken down but not completely smooth. Transfer to a bowl and set aside.

2   Put the cashews with their soaking water into a blender and blend until very smooth. Transfer to a bowl and set aside.

3   Heat the oil in a saucepan over medium-high heat. Add the cinnamon stick, mustard seeds, and asafetida (if using), and heat until the seeds begin to spatter, about 30 seconds. Add the garlic (if using), ginger, chili, and curry leaves (if using), and stir constantly until fragrant, about 30 seconds. Cover, if needed, to contain the spatter.

4   Add the corn kernels, coriander, cumin, turmeric, and salt, mix well, and reduce the heat to medium. Add ¼ cup (60 ml) water and cook for 10 minutes, until thickened, stirring frequently to prevent the mixture from sticking to the bottom of the pan.

5   Stir in the blended cashews and cook until thoroughly incorporated, 2 minutes, stirring frequently. Add water as needed to maintain a porridge-like consistency.

6   Remove from the heat, then add lime juice and salt to taste. Top with chopped cilantro and a sprinkling of sev, if desired. Prepare yourself for a hug in a bowl. Enjoy it while it's warm.

Hāndvo

SERVES 6 TO 8

Hāndvo is a savory Gujarāti cake made from a hearty and satiating blend of rice, lentils, legumes, and vegetables. Like with brownies, you'll find some people fighting for the crisp edges, while others prefer the tender middle. There are numerous versions of this dish, and each family has its own variation. My aunt Shanta Masi is our family's resident hāndvo maker, and her recipe was the inspiration for this one. Because the amount of vegetables will affect the texture of the final product, I recommend using a kitchen scale to weigh them. Although this recipe is simple to prepare, it does require preparation 1 to 2 days in advance, to soak the rice and legumes, blend, and then ferment the batter before baking. Hāndvo is even more delicious with green chutney (see page 212). Growing up, we'd also enjoy hāndvo with ketchup, a very American condiment which has become quite popular in India as well.

PREP TIME 12 TO 24 HOURS
BAKE TIME 35 MINUTES

HĀNDVO

1¼ cups (200 g) white bāsmati rice

¾ cup (150 g) split chanā dāl

¼ cup (50 g) split urad dāl

2½ cups (250 g) shredded cabbage (about ¼ medium head)

2 cups (400 g) grated zucchini and yellow squash (1 of each)

6 garlic cloves, minced (1½ tablespoons), optional

1 green chili, minced

1 tablespoon fresh lemon juice

2½ teaspoons salt

2 teaspoons cane sugar

1½ teaspoons grated ginger

¾ teaspoon ground turmeric

¼ teaspoon ground red chili, optional

VAGHĀR (TEMPERING)

3 tablespoons neutral oil, such as sunflower, plus more as needed

3 teaspoons black mustard seeds

¼ teaspoon asafetida

14 fresh curry leaves, torn, optional

½ teaspoon Eno fruit salt or baking soda

1½ tablespoons white sesame seeds

Green chutney (see page 212) and/or ketchup

1 Rinse and soak the rice and dāls together, covered in plenty of warm water, for at least 4 hours or overnight. Drain and add the rice and dāls to a blender along with 1 cup (240 ml) water. Blend until a slightly coarse batter (similar to wet sand) forms.

2 Transfer the batter to a large bowl, cover with a plate, and place in a warm spot (such as in the oven with the oven light on) to ferment for 8 to 10 hours, until risen slightly and almost fluffy in appearance.

3 Add the cabbage, squash, garlic (if using), green chili, lemon juice, salt, sugar, ginger, turmeric, and red chili to the batter and stir well to combine. Allow the batter to rest until loosened to a thick cake-batter consistency, about 30 minutes.

4 While the batter is resting, preheat the oven to 425°F (220°C). Lightly grease and line a 9 x 13 x 2-inch (23 x 33 x 5 cm) baking pan with parchment paper.

5 To prepare the vaghār (tempering), in a small pot, heat the oil over medium-high heat. Add the mustard seeds and cook until they begin to spatter, about 30 seconds. Remove from the heat and immediately add the asafetida and curry leaves (cover, if needed, to contain their excitement). Add half of the oil mixture to the batter along with the Eno fruit salt. Mix thoroughly to combine. Pour the batter into the prepared pan.

6 Spread the remaining oil mixture evenly onto the batter, ensuring that the mustard seeds are evenly distributed. Sprinkle the top with sesame seeds and bake for about 35 minutes, until an inserted toothpick comes out mostly clean. It is better to underbake rather than overbake it, as the hāndvo may become dry if cooked for too long.

7 If the top is not already deep brown, put the hāndvo under the broiler for 1 to 2 minutes.

8 Remove from the oven and allow the hāndvo to cool in the pan for about 1 hour. Cut and serve with green chutney and/or ketchup.

Zucchini Muthiyā

SERVES 4

My bā (paternal grandmother) and every one of her culinary creations were loved and adored by everyone around her. This muthiyā pays tribute to one of her most requested specialties. It's essentially a steamed dumpling made from āttā, the same flour used to make Rotli (an everyday flatbread, page 155). The dumplings are sliced and sautéed with seeds to enhance their bite and add depth of flavor. My bā always used zucchini from our neighbor's garden in the summer months to make them, but muthiyā can also be made with other vegetables, such as carrots and cabbage. I advise mastering this recipe with zucchini first before experimenting to your heart's desire.

PREP TIME 10 MINUTES
COOK TIME 1 HOUR

1 cup (200 g) grated zucchini
(1 medium zucchini)

¾ teaspoon salt

1 cup plus 2 tablespoons (145 g)
āttā or whole wheat pastry flour

¼ cup (50 g) ravo or semolina
flour

2½ teaspoons cane sugar

½ teaspoon ground turmeric

¼ teaspoon baking soda

1½ teaspoons grated ginger

2 garlic cloves, grated, optional

½ green chili, seeded and minced

1 tablespoon fresh lemon juice
(about ½ lemon)

Neutral oil, such as sunflower, as
needed

VAGHĀR (TEMPERING)

1 to 2 tablespoons neutral oil, such
as sunflower

¾ teaspoon black mustard seeds

2 teaspoons white sesame seeds

10 fresh curry leaves, torn, optional

Freshly chopped cilantro, optional

Green chutney (see page 212),
optional

Unsweetened plain nondairy
yogurt (see page 223), optional

Ketchup, optional

1 Mix the zucchini with salt and let stand until the liquid has been extracted, about 10 minutes.

2 Prepare a steamer pot (a large pot/Dutch oven with a lid). Place a steaming ring or ramekin in the center and fill the bottom of the pot with a few inches of water (keep the water level below the top of the steaming ring). Bring the water to a boil, reduce the heat to maintain a gentle simmer, and cover.

3 Whisk together the āttā, ravo, sugar, turmeric, and baking soda in a large bowl. Add the zucchini (with liquid), ginger, garlic (if using), green chili, and lemon juice. Combine to form a very loose dough that will still hold its shape. Add water or āttā as needed to maintain this consistency.

4 Using lightly oiled hands, form the dough into logs about 1 inch (2.5 cm) in diameter and length, depending on what you can fit on your steaming tray. Place the logs about 1 inch (2.5 cm) apart onto a lightly oiled perforated stainless-steel steaming dish. Steam until an inserted toothpick comes out clean, 15 to 20 minutes. Avoid opening the steamer before 15 minutes have passed. Work in batches if needed.

5 Carefully transfer the muthiyā logs onto a plate using tongs and cover with a clean, damp kitchen towel. Allow to cool for at least 30 minutes, then cut the logs into ½-inch (13 mm) disks.

6 To prepare the vaghār (tempering), heat the oil in a large nonstick pan over medium-high heat. Add the mustard seeds and heat until they pop, 30 seconds. Lower the heat and add the sesame seeds and curry leaves (if using). Stir for about 30 seconds, then add the muthiyā disks. Increase the heat to medium-high and cook until browned, 3 to 5 minutes, stirring frequently. Add 3 to 4 tablespoons of water and stir well until combined to ensure the muthiyā do not dry out.

7 Serve immediately, topped with cilantro, chutney, yogurt, or ketchup, as desired.

Khaman

SERVES 4 TO 6

Khaman is an iconic dish of Gujarāti cuisine. It's a savory steamed cake typically made from chanā dāl (split Bengal gram) or its flour. I've used the flour here for easy and quick preparation. This is sometimes also known as nylon khaman due to its light and fluffy texture. Eno fruit salt, available at Indian grocers or online, provides leavening that is essential for this recipe. I have tried to use baking soda and baking powder as substitutes for Eno fruit salt here, but I haven't had any luck with them.

PREP TIME 5 MINUTES
COOK TIME 45 MINUTES

KHAMAN

Neutral oil, such as sunflower, for greasing

1½ cups (150 g) besan or chickpea flour

½ teaspoon ground ginger

¼ teaspoon ground turmeric

¾ teaspoon salt

1½ tablespoons fresh lemon juice (about ½ lemon)

1 teaspoon Eno fruit salt

VAGHĀR (TEMPERING)

2 teaspoons neutral oil

1 teaspoon black mustard seeds

Pinch of asafetida, optional

8 fresh curry leaves, optional but recommended

½ to 1 green chili, thinly sliced

2 teaspoons cane sugar

Green chutney (see page 212)

Freshly chopped cilantro, optional

Grated fresh coconut, optional

1 Prepare a steamer pot (a large pot/Dutch oven with a lid). Place a steaming ring or ramekin in the center and fill the bottom of the pot with a few inches of water (keep the water level below the top of the steaming ring). Bring the water to a boil, reduce the heat to maintain a gentle simmer, and cover.

2 Lightly grease an 8-inch (20 cm) round cake pan with oil.

3 In a large bowl, whisk together the besan, ginger, turmeric, salt, ¾ cup plus 1 tablespoon (200 ml) water, and lemon juice to form a thin batter. Just before steaming, vigorously whisk in the Eno fruit salt until just combined.

4 Pour the mixture into the greased cake pan and spread gently and evenly with a spoon. To ensure a light and fluffy final product, avoid tapping the pan.

5 Place the pan into the steamer atop the steaming ring, cover, and steam for 20 to 25 minutes, until an inserted toothpick comes out clean.

6 Remove the pan from the steamer and allow the khaman to rest for about 10 minutes in the pan.

7 While the khaman is resting, prepare the vaghār. Heat the oil in a small saucepan over medium-high heat. Add the mustard seeds and cook until they pop, about 30 seconds, then add the asafetida (if using). Remove from the heat and add the curry leaves (if using) and green chili, and stir for 30 seconds. Add ⅓ cup (80 ml) water and the sugar, and continue to mix until the sugar is dissolved.

8 Once the khaman has cooled, cut it into 2-inch (5 cm) squares. Pour the spiced water mixture evenly over the top and allow it to rest for 15 minutes.

9 Serve at room temperature with green chutney and top with cilantro and grated coconut, if desired.

VARIATION Sev Khamani is a dish made from crumbled khaman that can be enjoyed as a snack or savory breakfast. It's a great option for leftover khaman or if your khaman is too dry or moist. Simply allow the khaman to cool completely, then crumble with your hands. Top with sev (thin or nylon) along with more grated coconut and cilantro. Serve with green chutney.

IDADĀ

Idadā

SERVES 8

Idadā is a version of dhoklā, which encompasses a family of savory steamed cakes like Khaman (page 48). The difference here is that idadā are made from a batter of rice and lentils that's fermented to give them a subtle tang. This recipe is my mom's specialty. She tops it with freshly cracked black pepper and ground red chili for extra flavor. The fermentation process requires more patience than effort, so plan for this dish to be a two-day project, but it's mostly waiting. This batter can also be made in larger batches and frozen for up to six months. Simply defrost in the refrigerator the night before steaming.

PREP TIME 24 HOURS
COOK TIME 1 HOUR

1½ cups (300 g) medium grain white rice, such as Sonā Masuri

½ cup (100 g) split white urad dāl

¾ teaspoon salt

2 teaspoons Eno fruit salt

Neutral oil, such as sunflower and/ or cooking spray, for greasing

Freshly cracked black pepper, to taste

Ground red chili, to taste

Freshly chopped cilantro, optional

Cilantro Peanut Chutney (page 212), optional

Keri No Ras (page 170), optional

1 On the morning of the first day, soak the rice and dāl covered with plenty of water in a large bowl. Cover with a plate and leave at room temperature for 10 to 12 hours.

2 Later that day, drain the soaked ingredients and put them in a blender with ¾ cup (180 ml) water. Blend until mostly smooth and just barely coarse (similar to wet sand). Add additional water if needed to reach this consistency. Transfer to a large bowl, cover with a plate, and place in a warm spot (such as in oven with the oven light on) to ferment for 10 to 12 hours or overnight. Stir the salt into the fermented batter and set aside.

3 When ready to cook, prepare a steamer pot (a large pot/Dutch oven with a lid). Place a steaming ring or ramekin in the center and fill the bottom of the pot with a few inches of water (keep the water level below the top of the steaming ring). Bring the water to a boil, reduce the heat to maintain a gentle simmer, and cover.

4 Lightly grease an 8-inch (20 cm) round cake pan or stainless-steel steaming pan.

5 In a medium bowl, put about ¾ cup (160 to 180 g) batter (about one fourth of the batter). If needed, add water (1 tablespoon at a time) to make a runny cake-batter consistency.

6 Add ½ teaspoon Eno fruit salt to the batter and sprinkle about 1 teaspoon water over it. Whisk the batter vigorously until just combined, pour evenly onto the greased pan, and evenly sprinkle black pepper and ground red chili on top. Place into the steamer, cover, and steam for 12 to 15 minutes, until an inserted toothpick comes out clean.

7 Remove the cover, then brush or spray a thin layer of oil on the idadā to prevent it from getting too dry. Allow it to rest for about 5 minutes, then cut into 2-inch (5 cm) diamonds and transfer to an airtight container (see Storage Tip).

8 Work in batches to use up the remaining batter, which will fill 3 more pans. Serve warm or at room temperature, topped with cilantro and served with Cilantro Peanut Chutney or Keri No Ras, if desired.

NOTES

1 The idadā may come out too dry if the batter isn't blended well enough, the batter is too thick, it is steamed for too long, or the top isn't brushed with enough oil. Once you make your first tray, these glitches will become obvious, and you'll be able to troubleshoot to correct the next batch.

2 Turmeric (about ½ teaspoon) can be added to the batter with the salt, if desired. You can also add a sprinkling of cooked and mashed green peas and carrots on top of the batter before steaming.

STORAGE TIP After fermenting, the batter can be cooked right away or stored in the refrigerator for up to 5 days until ready to use. It can also be frozen in an airtight container for up to 6 months. Defrost overnight in the refrigerator and use within 1 to 2 days.

SOUPS
AND
SALADS

I ndian flavors and ingredients have inspired me to create the Westernized soups and salads in this chapter. The soups are warm and hearty, the salads are bright and refreshing, and either can be a welcome addition to the table depending on what you're craving. Some of them can be paired with other recipes in this book to create a complete meal. Pair Sweet Corn Soup (page 56) with Chili Cauliflower and Tofu (page 35) for an Indo-Chinese meal, or Quinoa Kachumber (page 60) with Shāhi Gobi (page 93) and Nān (page 164) for a North Indian spread. Others, like Garam Masālā and Pāpad Salad (page 63), with some modifications or additions, can even be enjoyed as a full meal on their own.

Sweet Corn Soup

SERVES 4

This Indo-Chinese-inspired soup gets its warmth from the combination of aromatics and the addition of cumin, which offers earthy undertones. It comes together in a cinch and can easily become a heartier meal by adding diced firm tofu or noodles. I prefer a higher veg-to-broth ratio when it comes to brothy soups like this, but feel free to add more broth if you like.

PREP TIME 10 MINUTES
COOK TIME 20 MINUTES

1 tablespoon extra virgin olive oil

½ teaspoon freshly cracked black pepper, plus more for serving

4 scallions, thinly sliced into white and green parts

1 large carrot, diced (about ½ cup/60 g)

2 celery stalks, diced (about ⅓ cup/45 g)

Pinch of salt, plus more as needed

6 garlic cloves, minced or crushed (about 1½ tablespoons)

1 teaspoon grated ginger

1½ teaspoons ground cumin

1½ cups (200 g) frozen corn

½ cup (65 g) frozen green peas

3 cups (720 ml) low-sodium vegetable broth

2 tablespoons low-sodium soy sauce

2 teaspoons rice vinegar

1½ teaspoons sriracha, or to taste

Freshly chopped cilantro

1 Heat the oil in a large saucepan over medium heat until glossy. Swirl in the pepper and stir until fragrant, about 30 seconds. Increase the heat to medium-high. Add the white scallion parts, carrot, and celery, sprinkle with salt, and cook, stirring occasionally, until the vegetables start to soften, about 3 minutes.

2 Add the garlic, ginger, and cumin. Stir until fragrant, about 30 seconds, then add the corn and peas, and continue to stir until they start to soften, 5 minutes. Add the broth and soy sauce and bring to a boil. Reduce the heat to medium-low and simmer uncovered until the vegetables are tender, about 10 minutes.

3 Stir in the vinegar, sriracha, and more salt if needed to adjust to taste.

4 Serve hot, topped with the green scallion parts and/or cilantro.

Creamy Masālā Tomato Soup

SERVES 4

My first experience with Indian tomato soup was on my first memorable trip to India when I was in high school. We were welcomed to Ahmedabad with a gathering of family members on the agāsi (terrace) of my cousin's home. It was winter and slightly chilly, so we were offered cups of hot tomato soup. Because of the addition of spices, the soup had much more depth of flavor, compared to the canned tomato soup I was used to at home in Wisconsin. This recipe makes a creamier version of the soup I enjoyed in India, with the addition of mint for brightness.

PREP TIME 15 MINUTES
COOK TIME 30 MINUTES

One 24-ounce (680 g) can whole peeled tomatoes (such as San Marzano)

1 teaspoon coriander seeds

1 teaspoon cumin seeds

½ teaspoon black peppercorns

½ teaspoon fennel seeds

1 teaspoon garam masālā (see page 232)

¼ teaspoon ground red chili, to taste

¼ teaspoon ground turmeric

½ cup (70 g) unsalted raw or roasted cashews, soaked in hot water for 15 minutes

¼ cup (20 g) packed fresh mint leaves

1 tablespoon extra virgin olive oil

6 garlic cloves, minced (about 1½ tablespoons)

1 tablespoon grated ginger

2 cups (480 ml) low-sodium vegetable broth

2 tablespoons nutritional yeast (see page 15), optional

Freshly chopped mint

Freshly cracked black pepper

Crusty bread, optional

1 Place the tomatoes in a large bowl, then break them into small chunks with your fingers. Set aside.

2 Coarsely grind the coriander, cumin, black peppercorns, and fennel seeds using a mortar and pestle or spice grinder. Stir in the garam masālā, red chili, and turmeric. Set aside.

3 Drain the cashews and place in a blender with ⅓ cup water (80 ml) and the fresh mint leaves. Blend until very smooth. Set aside.

4 Combine the oil, garlic, and ginger in a large saucepan over medium-high heat. Stir frequently until the aromatics begin to sizzle, 30 seconds. Lower the heat slightly and cook until starting to brown, 3 to 5 minutes.

5 Reduce the heat to low, add the ground spices, and stir for a few seconds to toast without burning them. Add the tomatoes and bring to a simmer. Reduce the heat slightly and continue to simmer until the tomatoes have softened, about 10 minutes.

6 Add the vegetable broth and nutritional yeast (if using). Simmer until reduced slightly, about 15 minutes, then stir in most of the cashew cream, reserving some for serving.

7 For a smoother soup, use an immersion blender or cool slightly and transfer to a blender to blend until smooth. Adjust the salt and chili to taste.

8 To serve, transfer to serving bowls and top with reserved mint cashew cream as well as fresh mint and black pepper. Serve with crusty bread, if desired.

Quinoa Kachumber

SERVES 4

In northern India, the most common salad is generally known as kachumber. With crisp cucumbers, tomatoes, onions, and enticing chāt masālā (see page 236), it is a refreshing side to nearly any meal. I like to add quinoa for a nutritious boost of protein and fiber, but you can certainly omit it, and you can reduce the amount of lime juice and chāt masālā if you prefer the salad in its simplest form. Cooked amaranth or farro may also be used in place of quinoa, if desired. This salad is best enjoyed in the summer, when tomatoes and cucumbers are at their peak, but it is typically eaten year-round.

PREP TIME 15 MINUTES
COOK TIM: 15 MINUTES

⅓ cup (60 g) quinoa (any color)

½ English cucumber, finely diced

1 plum tomato, seeded and finely diced

½ small bell pepper, finely diced

½ small red onion, finely diced, optional

3 tablespoons finely chopped cilantro or mint

Juice of ½ lime (about 1 tablespoon), or to taste

½ to 1 teaspoon chāt masālā (see page 236)

1 Rinse the quinoa thoroughly under cold running water. Combine the quinoa and ⅔ cup (160 ml) water in a saucepan and bring to a boil. Reduce the heat to a gentle simmer, cover, and cook for 15 minutes. Remove from the heat and cool to room temperature.

2 Combine the cooled quinoa with the cucumber, tomato, pepper, onion (if using), cilantro, lime juice, and chāt masālā in a large bowl, toss well, and adjust the lime juice and chāt masālā to taste. Serve immediately or chilled.

3 This salad keeps particularly well if you need to make it ahead of time. It stays fresh for up to 5 days if refrigerated in an airtight container.

VARIATION This salad can also be enjoyed atop crisp pāpad as a dish called masālā pāpad. Pāpad is a type of paper-thin cracker made from urad dāl that can be found at any Indian grocery or online. Simply roast it on the stovetop over a grate on medium-high heat, flipping frequently until evenly bubbly and crisp, 30 to 60 seconds. Top the pāpad with the kachumber and a sprinkling of chāt masālā and cilantro.

Garam Masālā and Pāpad Salad

SERVES 2 AS A MEAL OR 4 AS A SIDE

This salad gets its Indian flair from garam masālā (page 232) and roasted pāpad, a crisp lentil cracker that can be found at any at any Indian grocer (and many international ones). I recommend enjoying this salad during late summer or early fall, but don't feel restricted by the seasons. Add cubes of tofu, chickpeas, or grilled tempeh to make this meal heartier.

PREP TIME 15 MINUTES

Half batch Garam Masālā Dressing (page 228), to taste

1 large carrot, cut into thin strips (see Prep Tip)

1 Persian cucumber, thinly sliced

3 ounces (85 g) mixed greens, torn up

½ Honeycrisp apple, thinly sliced

2 tablespoons roughly chopped unsalted pistachios (roasted or raw)

1 tablespoon chopped golden raisins

1 tablespoon chopped mint

2 to 4 pieces roasted pāpad (see Ingredient Tip)

Pinch of chāt masālā (see page 236), optional

1 Place 1 tablespoon Garam Masālā Dressing in a large mixing bowl. Add the carrot and cucumber and mix until thoroughly coated.

2 Add the greens and apple and toss gently with clean hands (or tongs). Taste and adjust the amount of dressing.

3 Place the salad on a serving plate and top with the pistachios, raisins, and mint. Crush the roasted pāpad on top and serve immediately, with a dusting of chāt masālā, if desired.

PREP TIP Use a mandoline to slice the cucumber and apple and a julienne peeler for the carrot if you can, as these tools yield even cuts. A sharp chef's knife can also do the same.

INGREDIENT TIP I prefer South Indian-style pāpad, called appalam, for this recipe. It is thicker and holds up better in the salad. Pretty much any variety of pāpad works fine (see page 60, Variation), or it can be omitted.

Citrus, Fennel, and White Bean Salad

SERVES 2 AS A MEAL OR 4 AS A SIDE

Having lived in the Midwest my entire life, I am certainly not a stranger to frigid and dark winters. This salad is designed to uplift and rejuvenate during the coldest of months, which also happens to be when citrus fruits are in season and in their most luscious state. I like to think of it as an ode to citrus and fennel. The recipe features the whole fennel plant, from seed to bulb to frond, and marries it with vibrant citrus.

PREP TIME 10 MINUTES
COOK TIME 5 MINUTES

½ teaspoon coriander seeds

½ teaspoon fennel seeds

1 small fennel bulb
(about 1 cup/85 g), sliced
paper thin

One 15-ounce (425 g) can white
beans, such as cannellini or
great northern, drained and
rinsed

1 grapefruit, peeled and
segmented

2 oranges, such as navel or Cara
Cara, peeled and segmented

Juice of ¼ lime (1 to 2 teaspoons),
or to taste

2 teaspoons extra virgin olive oil

1 teaspoon date syrup or desired
sweetener, optional

Pinch of flaky salt, to taste

Fennel fronds

Freshly chopped mint

1 Toast the coriander and fennel seeds in a small dry pan over medium heat until fragrant and lightly browned, about 2 minutes. Allow to cool, then crush gently in a mortar or a spice grinder, allowing some seeds to remain whole. Set aside.

2 Spread the sliced fennel bulb in a thin layer on a serving dish. Top with the white beans and segmented grapefruit and orange.

3 Drizzle the lime juice, olive oil, and date syrup (if using) evenly over the salad. Sprinkle on the crushed coriander and fennel seeds and a pinch of salt. Garnish with fennel fronds and mint and serve immediately.

SHĀK
Vegetable Dishes

Shāk, also known as sabji/sabzi in Hindi, is a Gujarāti term for an everyday stir-fried vegetable dish served alongside any combination of dāl (lentils), bhāt (rice), and rotli (bread). The recipes here are primarily drawn from the Gujarāti and North Indian preparations I've grown up with. Flāvar Vatānā Nu Shāk (page 68) and Tindorā (page 87) are ones I fondly remember enjoying with my bā and other family members both at home and in India. I've also included a South Indian dish, called poriyal in Tamil, that I've come to enjoy in recent years. It incorporates curry leaves, coconut, and urad dāl—lovely, nutty flavors not usually found in North Indian vegetable dishes. All the dishes in this chapter truly celebrate the vegetables used. Various spices enhance their natural flavors, while also adding antioxidants and anti-inflammatory properties to an already extremely healthful and fiber-rich food.

Flāvar Vatānā Nu Shāk

SERVES 2 TO 4

Flāvar is a Gujarāti term for cauliflower, which is paired with green peas in this classic recipe. I call for roasting the cauliflower because roasting truly transforms it and accentuates its wonderful texture and flavor. This shāk is best served with Rotli (page 155) or Parāthā (page 159), but it's also delicious on its own or mixed with Whole Moong Dāl (page 117) and rice.

PREP TIME 5 MINUTES
COOK TIME 45 MINUTES

ROASTED CAULIFLOWER

1 large head of cauliflower (800 g to 1 kg), cut into bite-size florets

1 tablespoon olive oil

½ teaspoon ground turmeric

¼ teaspoon salt

SHĀK

1½ teaspoons olive oil

1 teaspoon cumin seeds

1 teaspoon grated ginger

10 fresh curry leaves, optional

Pinch of asafetida, optional

¾ cup (100 g) frozen peas

Pinch of salt, plus more as needed

1 teaspoon ground coriander

¼ to ½ teaspoon ground red chili

1 to 2 teaspoons lime juice (from ½ lime)

Freshly chopped cilantro

1 Preheat the oven to 450°F (230°C). Line a baking sheet with parchment paper.

2 Place the cauliflower in a large bowl along with the oil, turmeric, and salt. Massage the oil into the florets so that each piece is evenly coated. Spread onto the baking sheet and roast for 35 to 40 minutes, until very tender and charred.

3 To finish making the shāk, heat the oil in a wok or wide pan over medium-high heat. Add the cumin seeds and heat until they start to turn deeper brown in color, about 30 seconds. Lower the heat to medium-low, stir in the ginger, curry leaves (if using), and asafetida (if using), and stir for a few seconds. Cover briefly if needed to contain any spattering.

4 Add the peas along with a pinch of salt and stir-fry until tender and heated through, about 3 minutes. Add the cauliflower and heat until well combined, about 2 minutes.

5 Add the coriander and red chili and stir for a few seconds. Add ¼ cup (60 ml) water and continue stirring until most of the water has evaporated, 2 to 3 minutes. Mash some of the peas and cauliflower, stir well, then remove from the heat.

6 Stir in the lime juice and additional salt if needed, to taste. Garnish with cilantro.

Butternut Squash Chanā Nu Shāk

SERVES 4 TO 6

Dudhi chanā nu shāk is a Gujarāti dish that is a specialty of my mom's. Comforting and hearty, it consists of dudhi or bottle gourd (a neutral-flavored, honeydew-green oval squash) cooked with split Indian chickpeas (chanā dāl). This version uses butternut squash, which gives the dish a welcome sweetness. Other squash, such as acorn or delicata, or the traditional bottle gourd may also be used in this recipe. Serve with beet rotli (see page 157) or rice.

PREP TIME 12 HOURS
COOK TIME 30 MINUTES

⅓ cup (65 g) chanā (split Bengal gram), rinsed and soaked in plenty of water overnight

1 tablespoon extra virgin olive oil

1 teaspoon cumin seeds

¼ teaspoon carom seeds, optional

Pinch of asafetida, optional

4 garlic cloves, minced (about 1 tablespoon)

1 tablespoon grated ginger

1 medium butternut squash, cut into ¾-inch (2 cm) chunks (4 to 5 cups/525 to 650 g)

½ teaspoon ground turmeric

Pinch of ground red chili, plus more to taste

1¼ teaspoons salt

1 teaspoon garam masālā (see page 232)

Fresh lime juice, optional

Freshly chopped cilantro, optional

1 Drain the soaked chanā and set aside.

2 Heat the oil in a large pot or Dutch oven over medium-high heat. Add the cumin and carom seeds and heat until they start to brown, a few seconds. Lower heat to medium-low.

3 Add the asafetida (if using), garlic, and ginger, and stir for a few seconds. Add the chanā and 2 cups (480 ml) water and stir well to combine. Bring to a boil, lower the heat to medium-low, cover, and cook for about 10 minutes or until the chanā starts to become tender.

4 Add the squash, turmeric, red chili, and salt. Stir well to combine, cover, and continue to cook until the squash is tender, about 20 minutes. Stir in the garam masālā and adjust to taste.

5 To serve, squeeze on the lime juice and garnish with cilantro, if desired.

Methi Batākā Nu Shāk

SERVES 2 TO 4

This preparation of potatoes with methi (fenugreek leaves) comes from my mother-in-law. The aromatic and slightly bitter methi pairs perfectly with the spiced potatoes and crunchy cashews. If you can't find methi, feel free to substitute cilantro or even spinach. Serve with Theplā (page 163) or Khichadi (page 140).

PREP TIME 10 MINUTES
COOK TIME 25 MINUTES

1 tablespoon neutral oil, such as sunflower

1 teaspoon cumin seeds

½ teaspoon black mustard seeds

2 garlic cloves, minced (about 1½ teaspoons), optional

1 teaspoon grated ginger

Pinch of asafetida, optional

2 russet potatoes, peeled if desired and cut into ¾-inch (2 cm) chunks

½ teaspoon salt, plus more to taste

½ cup (38 g) fresh methi (fenugreek leaves), roughly chopped

1 teaspoon ground coriander

½ teaspoon ground cumin

¼ teaspoon ground turmeric

¼ teaspoon ground red chili, to taste

¼ cup (35 g) roasted cashews

Fresh lime juice, to taste

1 Heat the oil in a wok or wide pan over medium-high heat. Add the cumin and mustard seeds and heat until the mustard seeds begin to spatter, about 30 seconds.

2 Add the garlic (if using), ginger, and asafetida (if using), and continue to cook until fragrant, a few seconds longer.

3 Add the potatoes and salt, lower the heat slightly, and continue to cook, stirring frequently, until the potatoes start to brown, 6 to 8 minutes.

4 Pour in 1 cup (240 ml) water, cover, lower the heat to medium-low, and continue to cook until the potatoes are fork-tender, 8 minutes.

5 Remove the lid and increase the heat to medium. Add the methi, coriander, cumin, turmeric, and red chili, and stir until the methi has cooked down slightly and most of the water has evaporated, 2 to 4 minutes.

6 To serve, stir in the roasted cashews, adjust the salt to taste, and squeeze on the lime juice to taste.

Roasted Bhindā

SERVES 2 TO 4

Bhindā, or okra, can be divisive. Some people adore it, while others strongly dislike it. I was previously in the latter category until I developed this recipe for my okra-loving wife, Rachel. I cut the okra into thin strips, then roast it until it's charred and chewy, a process that eliminates the sometimes slimy texture that once turned me off. If you're on the fence about this vegetable, this recipe may be the one to make it part of your regular rotation. I like serving it atop a piping hot bowl of Tadkā Dāl (page 110) and rice.

PREP TIME 10 MINUTES
COOK TIME 30 MINUTES

10 ounces (300 g) okra, quartered lengthwise into strips

1 tablespoon neutral oil, such as sunflower

Pinch of salt, plus more to taste

1 teaspoon ground coriander

1 to 2 garlic cloves, grated (about 1 teaspoon), optional

1 teaspoon grated ginger

½ teaspoon cumin seeds

¼ to ½ teaspoon ground red chili

¼ teaspoon āmchur (dried green mango powder), optional

¼ teaspoon ground turmeric

Pinch of carom seeds, optional

Pinch of asafetida, optional

1 Preheat the oven to 425°F (220°C). Line a large baking sheet with parchment paper.

2 Place the okra in a large mixing bowl with the oil and salt. Massage the oil into the okra so that each piece is evenly coated. Place in a single layer on the baking sheet, then roast for about 20 minutes or until the okra has just started to brown.

3 Transfer the okra to a bowl and toss in the coriander, garlic (if using), ginger, cumin seeds, red chili, āmchur, turmeric, carom seeds (if using), and asafetida (if using). Transfer back to the pan in a single layer.

4 Return the pan to the oven for about 5 minutes or until the okra starts to char. Remove from the oven and adjust the salt to taste.

Ringan Nā Palitā

SERVES 2 TO 4

Ringan Nā Palitā is a Gujarāti eggplant dish my wife, Rachel, and her family introduced me to when we were dating. I instantly fell in love with the tender coins of eggplant topped with a crisp masālā that is bursting with flavor. It's similar to a Bengāli dish called begun bhaja, which is also apt since my mother-in-law grew up in Kolkata. Serve with Rotli (page 155) or Parāthā (page 159).

PREP TIME 15 MINUTES
COOK TIME 25 MINUTES

2 tablespoons roasted peanuts

2 tablespoons grated coconut, fresh or thawed

1 teaspoon white sesame seeds

2 garlic cloves

1 teaspoon grated ginger

2 tablespoons roughly chopped cilantro

1 tablespoon plus ½ teaspoon oil

½ teaspoon lemon juice

1 teaspoon ground coriander

1 teaspoon ground cumin

½ teaspoon ground red chili

½ teaspoon ground turmeric

½ teaspoon cane sugar

½ teaspoon salt

1 Chinese eggplant (or preferred variety)

Freshly chopped cilantro, optional

1 In a mortar, smash the peanuts to form a paste. Add the coconut and sesame seeds and continue to pound until well combined. Add the garlic and ginger and mash, then add the cilantro. Stir in ½ teaspoon of the oil, lemon juice, coriander, cumin, chili, turmeric, sugar, and salt, and set aside. Alternatively, place all the spice ingredients in a small blender or food processor and pulse until well combined.

2 Slice the eggplant into ½-inch (13 mm) slices. Score one side of the eggplant slices by making four or five cuts halfway across the surface with a sharp knife. Spread a thin layer of the spice paste (½ to 1 teaspoon) onto the scored surface of each slice.

3 Heat a wide nonstick pan over medium heat. Add the remaining 1 tablespoon oil and put the eggplant slices in a single layer in the pan, spice-paste side up. Lower the heat to medium-low, cover, and cook until browned on the bottoms, 10 minutes.

4 Remove the lid, flip the eggplant slices, and continue to cook until the masālā side has browned, about 10 minutes. Work in batches if needed. Transfer the eggplant to a plate, masālā side up. Taste one slice for salt, and adjust the seasoning.

5 If the eggplant seems a bit undercooked, you can return the slices to the pan, masālā side up, sprinkle with water, cover, and cook over medium-low heat until softened, 5 to 10 minutes. Garnish with cilantro, if desired.

Green Bean Poriyal

SERVES 2 TO 4

Poriyal is a South Indian vegetable dish flavored with curry leaves, mustard seeds, and coconut (all readily available at Indian grocery stores). I also use split white urad dāl, which is widely used in South Indian cuisine for its nutty crunch. There are many ways of preparing it with nearly any vegetable, such as carrots, cabbage, and broccoli; I've used green beans here. Serve with Rotli (page 155), Sāmbār (page 114), or Lemon Rice (page 139).

PREP TIME 5 MINUTES
COOK TIME 10 MINUTES

1 tablespoon neutral oil, such as sunflower

1 teaspoon split white urad dāl

¼ teaspoon asafetida

1 teaspoon black mustard seeds

10 fresh curry leaves

12 ounces (340 g) green beans, sliced into ¼-inch (6 mm) pieces (about 3 cups)

½ teaspoon salt

½ cup (40 g) grated unsweetened coconut, fresh or frozen and thawed

Fresh lemon or lime juice

1 Heat the oil in a wide pan or wok over medium-high heat. Add the urad dāl and toast until it's just starting to turn very light brown, about 1 minute.

2 Add the asafetida and mustard seeds, and continue to heat until the mustard seeds begin to spatter. Remove from the heat, add the curry leaves, and cover immediately. Remove the cover once the spattering stops.

3 Return the pan to medium heat, stir in the green beans and salt, and stir-fry until well combined, about 1 minute. Add ¼ cup (60 ml) water, cover, and cook until the green beans are fully tender, about 8 minutes.

4 Remove the lid, stir in the coconut, and cook for 1 to 2 minutes to fully blend the flavors. Add salt if needed and remove from the heat. Stir in the lemon juice to taste and serve warm or at room temperature.

Sambhāro

SERVES 6 TO 8

Sambhāro is essentially a quickly cooked cabbage slaw. It uses only two vegetables and is served on a thāli to provide a crisp contrast to other more well-cooked vegetable dishes, such as Flāvar Vatānā Nu Shāk (page 68) or Ringan Nā Palitā (page 76). I like to make a larger batch of this to enjoy through the week as a side dish. Serve alongside other shāk dishes and Rotli (page 155) or with Gujarāti Dāl (page 113) and rice.

PREP TIME 10 MINUTES
COOK TIME 5 MINUTES

1 tablespoon olive oil

1 teaspoon black mustard seeds

1 green chili, thinly sliced

10 fresh curry leaves, optional but recommended

Pinch of asafetida, optional

6 cups (540 g) shredded green cabbage (about ½ small head)

2 cups (180 g) julienned carrots (about 2 medium carrots)

½ teaspoon ground turmeric

¾ teaspoon salt

1 teaspoon lime juice (about ½ small lime)

2 tablespoons chopped cilantro, optional

1   Heat the oil in a deep, wide pan or wok over medium-high heat. Add the mustard seeds and heat until they pop, about 30 seconds.

2   Lower the heat to low, then add the green chili, curry leaves (if using), and asafetida (if using). Cover, if needed, to contain the spatter. When the spattering stops, add the cabbage, carrots, turmeric, and salt, and stir well to combine.

3   Increase the heat to medium and stir until thoroughly combined and just slightly softened, about 3 minutes. For a softer texture, continue to cook for about 5 more minutes.

4   Remove from the heat, stir in the lime juice and cilantro (if using), and adjust salt to taste. Serve at room temperature or chilled.

VARIATION   Sambhāro can also be made with thinly sliced Brussels sprouts or red cabbage. When using red cabbage, I like to add about ½ teaspoon coarsely ground fennel seeds along with the mustard seeds, since the flavors work particularly well together.

Marchā Nu Shāk

SERVES 2 TO 4

When I was growing up, we had an elderly handyman (we'd affectionately call him kākā—"uncle" in Gujarāti—although he was German) who would come to do basic fixer-upping—one of his favorite activities to stay active. He and my bā (grandmother) developed a sweet friendship because he would bring large quantities of fresh peppers from his garden that she would make into bharelā marchā (peppers stuffed with a mouthwatering filling of peanuts, chickpea flour, sesame seeds, and spices). I developed this recipe with those flavors and memories in mind, but in a stir-fried and slightly quicker way. I like to serve this shāk along with Gujarāti Dāl (page 113) or Gujarāti Kadhi (page 121) and rice.

PREP TIME 5 MINUTES
COOK TIME 15 MINUTES

¼ cup (38 g) raw peanuts

3 tablespoons besan or chickpea flour

2 tablespoons white sesame seeds

1 tablespoon olive oil

1 large bell pepper and 1 banana pepper, diced into ½-inch (13 mm) chunks (about 3 cups/375 g), or peppers of your choice (see Ingredient Tip)

¼ teaspoon salt

1 teaspoon ground coriander

1 teaspoon ground cumin

¼ teaspoon ground turmeric

¼ teaspoon ground red chili

1 Grind the peanuts coarsely in a mortar or blender, then stir in the besan and sesame seeds. Transfer the mixture to a wide nonstick pan and toast it over medium heat, stirring constantly, until nutty and lightly browned, about 5 minutes. This can burn quickly, so watch carefully and lower the heat if needed. Transfer the mixture to a bowl and set aside.

2 In the same pan, heat the oil over medium heat. Add the peppers and salt, and cook, stirring occasionally, until softened and browned, about 5 minutes.

3 Lower the heat to medium-low, stir in the peanut mixture and coriander, cumin, turmeric, and red chili. Stir until well combined, 1 to 2 minutes. Add 3 tablespoons water and stir until the besan becomes clumpy and toasted, about 3 minutes. Serve warm or at room temperature.

INGREDIENT TIP I use a combination of bell pepper and banana pepper here since that's what kākā grew in his garden, but feel free to use whatever peppers, mild to spicy, that you prefer.

Rasāvālā Baby Potatoes with Greens

SERVES 4 TO 6

Rasāvālā is a descriptive term that refers to a saucier shāk, which is different from the drier shāks found in the rest of this chapter. The sauce is made with tomatoes, which give a brightness to the baby potatoes with greens. Kale, collard greens, spinach, or chard are all fair game. Serve with Rotli (page 155), Gobi Parāthā (page 160), or Theplā (page 163).

PREP TIME 5 MINUTES
COOK TIME 30 MINUTES

1 tablespoon extra virgin olive oil

½ teaspoon cumin seeds

½ teaspoon black mustard seeds

4 garlic cloves, minced (about 1 tablespoon)

1 tablespoon grated ginger

2 plum tomatoes, diced (about 1⅓ cups/210 g)

1 teaspoon salt

1 teaspoon ground coriander

1 teaspoon ground cumin

½ teaspoon ground red chili

½ teaspoon ground turmeric

1 pound (454 g) baby potatoes, cut into 1-inch (2.5 cm) chunks

3 cups (about 160 g) packed, roughly chopped greens, such as kale, collard greens, spinach, or chard

Freshly chopped cilantro

1 Heat the oil in a deep, wide pan or Dutch oven over medium-high heat. Add the cumin and mustard seeds and toast until the mustard seeds pop, about 30 seconds.

2 Reduce the heat to low, then stir in the garlic and ginger, and cook for a few seconds until fragrant. Add the tomatoes and salt, increase the heat to medium, and cook until the tomatoes start to soften, about 3 minutes.

3 Add the coriander, cumin, red chili, and turmeric, and stir for a few seconds. Add the potatoes and 2 cups (480 ml) water, and bring to a gentle boil.

4 Lower the heat to medium-low to maintain a continuous simmer. Cover and cook until the potatoes are fork-tender, about 15 minutes.

5 Mash some of the potatoes with the back of a spoon to release some of their starch to thicken the sauce. Remove the lid, increase the heat to medium-high, and continue to cook until thickened, about 5 minutes.

6 Add the greens and stir until wilted, about 1 minute. Adjust the salt and garnish with cilantro.

Tindorā

SERVES 4

Tindorā, also known as gilodā or ivy gourd, are slender, pale-green gourds that make one of my favorite childhood shāks. The tindorā is cooked until it's just tender but retains some bite; then it's stir-fried with a classic combination of spices. Tindorā can be found at Indian grocers (fresh tindorā cooks better than frozen), but if unavailable, fresh green beans (halved lengthwise) may be substituted.

PREP TIME 15 MINUTES
COOK TIME 30 MINUTES

1 pound (454 g) fresh tindorā

1½ tablespoons neutral oil, such as sunflower or grapeseed

¾ teaspoon cumin seeds

¾ teaspoon black mustard seeds

2 teaspoons grated ginger

Pinch of asafetida, optional

½ teaspoon salt, plus more to taste

½ teaspoon ground coriander

½ teaspoon ground cumin

½ teaspoon garam masālā
(see page 232)

¼ teaspoon ground red chili, plus more to taste

¼ teaspoon ground turmeric

2 teaspoons finely chopped jaggery or sugar

1 to 2 teaspoons fresh lime juice (from about ½ lime)

Freshly chopped cilantro, optional

1 Trim the ends of the tindorā. Slice each tindorā in half lengthwise, then slice each half once or twice to make thinner slices. Discard any pieces of tindorā that are red on the inside. Set aside.

2 Heat the oil in a deep, wide nonstick pan over medium-high heat. Add the cumin and mustard seeds and toast until the mustard seeds pop, about 30 seconds.

3 Reduce the heat to low, stir in the ginger and asafetida (if using), and continue to stir until fragrant, about 30 seconds.

4 Add the sliced tindorā and salt, and increase the heat to medium. Cover and continue cooking until the tindorā is tender and starting to brown, 20 to 25 minutes. Stir about every 5 minutes to prevent the tindorā from sticking to the bottom of the pan or burning.

5 Remove the cover, stir in the coriander, cumin, garam masālā, chili, and turmeric, and continue to cook for about 1 minute to toast (but not burn) the spices.

6 Remove from the heat, stir in the jaggery and fresh lime juice, and garnish with cilantro, if desired.

GRAVY
DISHES

The word "curry" is commonly used outside of India to describe hundreds of different dishes with their own nuances, but "gravy" is the term more commonly used by Indians to describe dishes that consist of a spiced sauce. I've included my versions of the gravies that are commonly served in Indian restaurants in the US (e.g., Shāhi Gobi, page 93), with modifications that make them fully plant-based but just as rich and hearty as the originals. These gravies can be served with breads, such as Nān (page 164), or rice (see page 126), which are both equally effective at mopping up their comforting goodness.

Mattar Tofu

SERVES 4

This gravy dish is typically made from peas and paneer (a soft Indian cheese) in a sometimes creamy onion and tomato gravy. This is my wife Rachel's absolute favorite Indian dish, and she has pretty high standards for it. I've been trying to make a vegan version that lived up to her criteria, and after three years, I can finally say I've accomplished it with this tofu version (she approved this statement, too!). The tomato masālā base can be made in advance, but for this recipe, I recommend pressing the tofu and soaking the cashews while making the masālā to save time. Enjoy with rice, Nān (page 164), or Parāthā (page 159).

PREP TIME 30 TO 60 MINUTES
COOK TIME 20 MINUTES

⅓ cup (50 g) raw cashews, soaked in hot water for 15 minutes

1 tablespoon olive oil

½ teaspoon cumin seeds

¼ teaspoon fennel seeds

One 14-ounce (400 g) block extra-firm tofu, drained and pressed for 30 to 60 minutes and cut into ¾-inch (2 cm) cubes (see Ingredient Tip)

Salt

¾ cup (100 g) frozen peas

1 batch Tomato Onion Masālā (page 240)

1 tablespoon dried fenugreek (kasoori methi) leaves

1 tablespoon nutritional yeast (see page 15), optional

Frozen peas, thawed, optional

Freshly chopped cilantro, optional

1 Prepare the cashew cream: Drain and blend the cashews with ⅓ cup (80 ml) water until very smooth. Set aside.

2 Heat the oil in a wide nonstick pan or braiser over medium heat. Add the cumin and fennel seeds and stir until fragrant, a few seconds. Add the tofu along with a generous pinch of salt and cook, stirring occasionally, until lightly browned on most sides, about 10 minutes.

3 Add 1 cup (240 ml) water, the peas, Tomato Onion Masālā, most of the cashew cream (reserve 2 to 3 tablespoons for serving), fenugreek leaves, and nutritional yeast (if using). Stir well to combine.

4 Cover and simmer over medium-low heat until well combined, about 10 minutes. Add additional water as needed to achieve the desired consistency and adjust salt to taste.

5 Serve topped with reserved cashew cream and garnished with a few peas and cilantro, if desired.

INGREDIENT TIP Use a tofu press for best results, but if not available, you can place the tofu between two paper towels or clean kitchen towels. Place a flat plate or cutting board on top of the tofu and a few heavy cans (like beans or soup) on top of the plate.

Shāhi Gobi

SERVES 4 TO 6

Shāhi, which means "royal" in Hindi, is a rich gravy preparation of Mughlai (Moghul) origin. The richness in this recipe comes from a golden-colored shāhi cream made from nuts, cardamom, saffron, and rose water. I pair this gravy with cauliflower that is roasted, charred, and buttery-tender. Feel free to pair it with any of your favorite vegetables, tofu, or chickpeas. Serve with plain rice, Nān (page 164), or Parāthā (page 159).

PREP TIME 5 MINUTES
COOK TIME 45 MINUTES

SHĀHI CREAM
¼ cup (40 g) raw cashews

¼ cup (36 g) raw almonds

3 green cardamom pods

½ teaspoon rose water

¼ teaspoon saffron

ROASTED CAULIFLOWER
1 large head cauliflower, cut into florets (about 28 ounces/800 g)

1 tablespoon olive oil

½ teaspoon ground turmeric

¼ teaspoon salt

GRAVY
1 batch Tomato Onion Masālā (page 240)

1 tablespoon nutritional yeast (see page 15), optional

2 teaspoons golden raisins

¼ teaspoon garam masālā (see page 232)

¼ teaspoon ground red chili, plus more to taste

¼ teaspoon salt, plus more to taste

SERVING
Almonds, chopped

Cashews, chopped

Cilantro, roughly chopped, optional

1 Preheat the oven to 450°F (230°C).

2 Soak the cashews and almonds in plenty of hot water and set aside.

3 Massage the cauliflower florets with oil, turmeric, and salt and place onto a large baking sheet in a single layer. Roast for 30 to 35 minutes, until starting to char.

4 When the cauliflower has nearly finished roasting, prepare the cashew and almond cream. Drain the cashews and almonds and blend with ½ cup (120 ml) water, the cardamom pods, rose water, and saffron. If not completely smooth, add 1 to 2 tablespoons water and continue to blend. If the mixture is still not silky, pass through a fine-mesh sieve. Set the resulting cream aside.

5 Combine the Tomato Onion Masālā, 1 cup (240 ml) water, nutritional yeast (if using), raisins, garam masālā, red chili, and salt in a wide pan or braising pan. Stir well to combine and bring to a simmer over medium heat.

6 Stir in most of the cashew and almond cream (reserve about 2 tablespoons for serving) and all of the cauliflower and simmer until well combined, about 5 minutes.

7 Add red chili and salt to taste.

8 Serve topped with the reserved cashew and almond cream, chopped almonds and cashews, and cilantro (if using).

Chhole/Chānā Masālā

SERVES 4 TO 6

The addition of mint and black tea to this gravy, a technique I learned from my Mumbai-native aunt Shruti Foi, is specifically designed to transform the humble chickpea into chhole. Chickpeas provide dietary fiber and play a role in modifying the gut microbiome,[26] so they are excellent for maintaining gut health. Black tea is used to cook dried chickpeas to give them a deeper color, but I use it primarily for depth of flavor. Mint provides a brightness that pairs well with the subtly bitter and astringent tea. Serve with rice or Parāthā (page 159) and Quinoa Kachumber (page 60).

PREP TIME 5 MINUTES
COOK TIME 25 MINUTES

Two 15.5-ounce (440 g) cans chickpeas, or about 3 cups precooked chickpeas

1 tablespoon loose-leaf black tea (or 2 to 3 tea bags)

1 batch Tomato Onion Masālā (page 240)

1 heaped tablespoon finely chopped fresh mint

¼ teaspoon baking soda

1 teaspoon garam masālā (see page 232)

¼ teaspoon black salt

Pinch of ground red chili, optional

¼ teaspoon smoked paprika

Pinch of āmchur (dried green mango powder), optional

½ teaspoon salt, plus more if needed

Finely chopped red onion, optional

Ginger, cut into matchsticks, optional

Chopped fresh cilantro or mint

1 Rinse and drain the chickpeas and set aside.

2 Steep the tea in 1 cup (240 ml) hot water for 5 minutes. Strain the tea and set aside.

3 Combine the chickpeas, tea, Tomato Onion Masālā, mint, and baking soda in a large saucepan or medium Dutch oven. Bring to a simmer over medium-high heat, then lower the heat slightly, cover, and cook until the chickpeas are very tender, about 20 minutes.

4 Mash some of the chickpeas and stir well. Add the garam masālā, black salt, red chili (if using), paprika, āmchur (if using), and additional salt to taste. Stir well to combine.

5 Serve hot, topped with finely chopped red onion, ginger, and cilantro, if desired.

Rājmā

SERVES 2 TO 4

Rājmā is a North Indian dish of kidney beans in a deeply nuanced gravy that pairs perfectly with jeerā rice (bāsmati rice cooked with cumin seeds). If the base masālā is made in advance, this dish comes together in a mere 15 minutes, the same time it takes to cook the rice.

PREP TIME 5 MINUTES
COOK TIME 15 MINUTES

One 15.5-ounce (440 g) can kidney beans, rinsed and drained

1 batch Smoky Tomato Onion Masālā (page 242)

1 tablespoon dried fenugreek (kasoori methi) leaves

1 teaspoon garam masālā (see page 232)

¼ teaspoon āmchur (dried green mango powder)

¼ teaspoon black salt

Salt, to taste

Ground red chili, to taste

Diced or sliced red onion

Ginger, cut into matchsticks, optional

Cilantro, optional

1 Combine the beans, tomato onion masālā, fenugreek leaves, and 1 cup (240 ml) water in a large saucepan. Simmer, partially covered, to let the flavors blend, 10 minutes.

2 Stir in the garam masālā, āmchur, black salt, salt, and red chili, adjusting the salt and red chili to taste.

3 Serve with red onion and with ginger and cilantro, if desired.

Navratan Kormā

SERVES 4

Navratan, or "nine gems," refers to the nine ingredients—fruits, nuts, and vegetables—added to this rich, luxurious, and traditionally vegetarian gravy. It starts with a gravy made from onions, nuts, and other aromatics that are boiled until tender, lending a natural sweetness and white color to the final gravy. It proves that a little sweetness can work quite well in savory dishes. Broccoli, tofu, and chickpeas also work really well with this gravy. You can use fewer ingredients or substitute your favorites. Serve with plain rice or Nān (page 164).

PREP TIME 5 MINUTES
COOK TIME: 35 MINUTES

GRAVY

1 yellow onion, roughly chopped (about 2 cups/300 g)

⅓ cup (50 g) raw cashews

¼ cup (36 g) raw almonds

1 tablespoon coriander seeds

1 tablespoon white poppy seeds, optional

1 bay leaf, optional

1 small piece mace, optional

4 green cardamom pods

½ teaspoon salt, plus more to taste

6 garlic cloves, minced (about 1½ tablespoons)

1 tablespoon minced ginger

½ green chili, minced, plus more to taste

NAVRATAN

1 tablespoon olive oil

½ teaspoon cumin seeds

½ teaspoon fennel seeds, optional

½ red bell pepper, diced (½ cup/75 g)

2 cups (100 g) bite-size cauliflower florets

1 medium carrot, diced (½ cup/70 g)

⅓ cup (45 g) fresh or frozen corn

⅓ cup (45 g) frozen peas, thawed

1 tablespoon golden raisins

½ teaspoon garam masālā (see page 232)

⅓ cup (50 g) diced fresh or frozen pineapple, thawed

Almonds, thinly sliced

Pistachios, thinly sliced

Cilantro, roughly chopped

1 For the gravy, combine the onion, cashews, almonds, coriander, poppy seeds (if using), bay leaf (if using), mace (if using), cardamom, and salt with 2 cups (480 ml) water in a large saucepan.

2 Bring to a boil, reduce the heat to a simmer, and cook until the onions are very soft, about 15 minutes. Add the garlic, ginger, and green chili, and cook until fragrant, about 1 minute.

3 Transfer the gravy mixture to a bowl or blender, cool slightly, remove the bay leaf, then blend until very smooth. Adjust the spiciness with more green chili to taste and blend again. Set aside.

4 To prepare the navratan, heat the oil in a large, wide pan over medium-high heat. Add the cumin and fennel seeds (if using) and heat until they start to turn a deeper brown, about 1 minute.

5 Add the bell pepper and sauté until it starts to soften, about 1 minute. Add the cauliflower, carrot, and a generous pinch of salt, and continue to sauté until they begin to brown, about 5 minutes.

6 Add the corn and peas and sauté until they start to become tender, 5 minutes. Add water, 1 tablespoon at a time, or lower the heat if the vegetables begin to stick to the bottom of the pan.

7 Stir in the gravy and raisins, reduce the heat to medium-low, cover, and simmer until all the veggies are tender, about 5 minutes.

8 Add water as needed until desired consistency is reached. Stir in the garam masālā and adjust the salt to taste.

9 Remove from the heat and top with the pineapple, almonds, pistachios, and cilantro.

Pālak Tofu

SERVES 4

This pālak (spinach)-based gravy proves that a gravy dish can be both hearty and refreshing at the same time. It's vibrant in color (due in part to the ice cubes added after cooking the spinach) and light, as it contains no nut-based cream. I recommend using garlic with a heavy hand in this recipe; the spinach will love it, and I trust you will, too. If you prefer a creamier version, you can stir in some cashew cream. And you can try adding chickpeas instead of tofu, to make a dish known as pālak chhole. Serve with Rotli (page 155), Parāthā (page 159), or plain rice.

PREP TIME 30 TO 60 MINUTES
COOK TIME 30 MINUTES

GRAVY

2 teaspoons olive oil

1 tablespoon coriander seeds

½ teaspoon cumin seeds

½ teaspoon fennel seeds

1 yellow onion, diced (about 2 cups/300 g)

½ teaspoon salt, plus more to taste

8 garlic cloves, minced (about 2 tablespoons)

1 tablespoon minced ginger

1 green chili, minced, plus more to taste

3 cups packed, roughly chopped spinach (about 5 ounces/140 g)

TURMERIC TOFU

1 tablespoon olive oil

One 14-ounce (400 g) block extra-firm tofu, drained and pressed for 30 to 60 minutes and cut into ¾-inch (2 cm) cubes (see Ingredient Tip on page 23)

½ teaspoon salt

½ teaspoon ground turmeric

1 teaspoon garam masālā (see page 232)

Juice of ½ lime (about 2 teaspoons), or to taste

1 Heat the oil in a wide pan or braising pan over medium heat. Add the coriander, cumin, and fennel seeds and heat until fragrant, about 1 minute.

2 Add the onion and salt, and stir occasionally until softened and starting to brown, 10 minutes. Adjust the heat between medium-low and medium to prevent the onions from browning too quickly.

3 Add the garlic, ginger, and green chili, and stir until very fragrant, 2 minutes. Add 1 cup (240 ml) water, increase the heat to medium-high, and bring to a simmer.

4 Add the spinach, stir, cover, and continue to cook until it has just started to wilt, about 2 minutes. Remove from the heat, transfer to a bowl or blender, and stir in 4 to 6 ice cubes to cool quickly.

5 Blend until smooth. This gravy can be chunkier or smoother according to your own preference. Set aside.

6 To prepare the tofu, heat the oil in a large, wide nonstick pan over medium heat. Add the tofu and salt, and cook, stirring occasionally until the tofu is lightly browned on most sides, about 10 minutes. Stir in the turmeric until the tofu pieces are evenly coated.

7 Pour the spinach gravy into the pan. Bring to a brief simmer over medium heat for 1 to 2 minutes, then remove from the heat. Stir in the garam masālā and lime juice and adjust the salt to taste.

VARIATION For a creamier version, soak ⅓ cup (50 g) cashews in hot water for 30 minutes, drain, then blend with ⅓ cup (80 ml) water until smooth. Add to the gravy in step 7 before simmering.

Sunflower Sāg with Black-Eyed Peas and Corn

SERVES 4

Sāg is a simple preparation of leafy greens. My version is creamy and hearty from the addition of a sunflower seed cream, which mellows the bitter notes of the kale. I serve it here with black-eyed peas and corn, but feel free to add tofu, other vegetables, or chickpeas instead. Serve this dish with rice or Rotli (page 155).

PREP TIME 5 MINUTES
COOK TIME 25 MINUTES

GRAVY

2 teaspoons neutral oil, such as sunflower

1 tablespoon coriander seeds

1½ teaspoons cumin seeds

1 yellow onion, diced (about 2 cups/300 g)

½ teaspoon salt

6 garlic cloves, minced or crushed (about 1½ tablespoons)

1 tablespoon minced ginger

1 green chili, minced

⅓ cup (45 g) hulled, roasted sunflower seeds (or use raw for a smoother sauce)

½ teaspoon ground turmeric

4 cups packed, roughly chopped kale (about 5 ounces/140 g)

SERVING

2 teaspoons neutral oil

1 cup (135 g) corn

One 15.5-ounce (440 g) can black-eyed peas, drained and rinsed

1 tablespoon nutritional yeast (see page 15), optional

1 teaspoon garam masālā (see page 232)

Juice of ½ lime (about 2 teaspoons), or to taste

Freshly chopped cilantro, optional

Sunflower seeds, for garnish

1 Heat the oil in a wide pan or braising pan over medium heat. Add the coriander and cumin seeds, and continue to heat until fragrant, about 1 minute.

2 Add the onion and salt, and stir occasionally, until the onion is softened and starting to brown, 10 minutes. Adjust the heat between medium-low and medium to prevent the onions from browning too quickly.

3 Reduce the heat to low, add the garlic, ginger, and chili, and stir until fragrant, 2 minutes. Stir in the sunflower seeds and turmeric, and add 1 cup (240 ml) water.

4 Increase the heat to medium and bring to a simmer. Add the kale, stir, cover, and continue to cook until the kale has wilted, 2 to 3 minutes. Remove from the heat and transfer to a bowl or blender, let cool for a few minutes, then blend until mostly smooth. Set aside.

5 Heat the oil over medium heat in the pan. Sauté the corn until it starts to soften, about 3 minutes.

6 Add the black-eyed peas, gravy, nutritional yeast (if using), and garam masālā, and simmer until well combined, 3 to 5 minutes. Add ¼ to ½ cup (60 to 120 ml) water as needed to reach the desired consistency.

7 Remove from the heat, adjust the salt to taste, squeeze on the lime juice, and garnish with cilantro and sunflower seeds, if desired.

Pāv Bhāji

SERVES 4

Pāv bhāji is a very popular street food, a stewed vegetable dish (bhāji) served with soft buttered rolls (pāv). The magic in this dish comes from pāv bhāji masālā, a spice blend that is available from Indian grocery stores. To avoid buying too many single-use spice blends, I make my own version with a mix of garam masālā (see page 232) and chāt masālā (see page 236). If you prefer to use store-bought pāv bhāji masālā, simply omit all the ground spices in this recipe and replace them with 2 to 3 teaspoons of pāv bhāji masālā.

PREP TIME 15 MINUTES
COOK TIME 40 MINUTES

3 cups (400 g) diced red potato (or preferred variety), peeled if desired

½ cup (68 g) frozen green peas

1 tablespoon vegan butter or olive oil

½ teaspoon cumin seeds

1 large red onion, finely diced (2½ cups/325 g)

1 red bell pepper, finely diced (1 cup/130 g)

½ teaspoon salt

6 garlic cloves, minced (about 1½ tablespoons)

1 tablespoon grated ginger

One 6-ounce (170 g) can tomato paste

1 teaspoon ground coriander

1 teaspoon garam masālā (see page 232)

2 teaspoons chāt masālā (see page 236)

1 teaspoon ground smoked paprika

½ teaspoon ground turmeric

¼ teaspoon ground red chili, plus more to taste

3 tablespoons nutritional yeast (see page 15), optional but recommended

Sliced red onion, for garnish

Freshly chopped cilantro, for garnish

Lime wedges, for garnish

Soft dinner rolls

Vegan butter or oil

1 Combine the potatoes and peas in a saucepan with 3½ cups (840 ml) water and bring to a boil. Reduce the heat, then simmer, uncovered, until the potatoes are fork-tender, 10 minutes. Mash the potatoes and peas together. This mixture will look quite liquidy. Set aside.

2 Heat the butter in a large, wide pan over medium-high heat. Add the cumin and stir for a few seconds, until fragrant, then add the onion, bell pepper, and ½ teaspoon salt, and sauté until softened and starting to brown, 10 to 15 minutes. Lower the heat and add water 1 tablespoon at a time, as needed, to prevent burning.

3 Lower the heat to medium-low. Add the garlic and ginger, stir for a few seconds, then add the tomato paste. Continue to cook until thick and fully heated through, about 3 minutes.

4 Add the coriander, garam masālā, chāt masālā, smoked paprika, turmeric, red chili, and nutritional yeast (if using), stir for a few seconds, then add the mashed potato and pea mixture. Reduce the heat to low, cover, and simmer until thoroughly combined and slightly thickened, about 5 minutes. Adjust the salt and red chili to taste. Garnish with red onion, cilantro, and lime wedges, and serve hot with toasted and buttered or oiled rolls.

PREP TIP Other vegetables may be used in addition to or in place of the potatoes and peas, including sweet potato, cauliflower, carrots, and corn. Simply boil until tender as in step 1 and proceed.

DĀL
Legume Stews

Dāl is an umbrella term for a comforting and hearty stew made from lentils, peas, or other legumes. This chapter contains the stews I grew up with and others I've come to adore. I've also included Gujarāti Kadhi (a yogurt-based stew, page 121) and Rasam (a tangy South Indian broth, page 122), which technically aren't dāl, but are similarly comforting. Most of these recipes are simple enough to make on a typical weeknight, but I suggest saving the Dāl Makhani (page 118) for special occasions, as it's more time-consuming. These dishes are delicious on their own, with plain rice, or with any preferred grain.

Making dāl might seem intimidating, but the process is quite straightforward. This false perception is based on dāl's cook time when made on the stovetop (the alternative is "whistle" stovetop pressure cookers, which I've never used due to my childhood fear of them*). These days, electric pressure cookers (such as the Instant Pot) are widely available and popular, and they make cooking dāl even easier. However, every recipe can be made on the stovetop, without a pressure cooker. It will just take a bit more time.

*I believe this fear to be justified, since I've heard more than one horror story of stovetop pressure cookers exploding. If you have and use one of these already, you probably don't need me to tell you anything about how to cook dāl. Use your own preferred method to cook the dāl itself, then proceed with the vaghār and other ingredients as listed in the individual recipes.

GENERAL TIPS FOR COOKING DĀL:

1   Dāl *loves* salt. Be sure to salt the dāl well to bring out its full flavor. Sometimes just a pinch more salt can take a pot of dāl from bland to vibrant.

2   Dāl cooking times can vary widely depending on the dāl's age, source, and other variables. The most important thing to note is that, unlike pasta, "al dente" is not a desired characteristic for dāl. Dāl should be very tender and falling apart. The starches will create a creaminess that needs no cream at all.

3   Don't skip out on the vaghār (tempered spices). Blooming spices in hot oil, to start and/or finish the dāl, is essential for allowing them to live their best lives in your dāl. More on this and other Indian cooking techniques on page 16.

4   The Indian Pantry (page 11) gives more information about the specific dāls and spices used in this chapter.

Tadkā Dāl

SERVES 4

Tadkā is an onomatopoeia, imitating the sizzle of tempered spices poured over piping hot cooked dāl. This is the basic recipe from which other types of dāl can be made. I call for split moong (split yellow mung beans) and/or masoor (split red lentils) since they are quick-cooking and readily available. Other types of dāl, such as chanā (split Indian chickpeas or Bengal gram) or tuver/toor dāl (split pigeon peas) may also be used, but they will take longer to cook. This dāl is delicious with or without the onions and garlic. Serve with rice or on its own.

PREP TIME 15 MINUTES
COOK TIME 40 MINUTES

DĀL

1 cup (about 200 g) split moong dāl or split masoor dāl, or a combination

2 teaspoons neutral oil, such as sunflower or avocado

½ yellow onion, finely diced (about 1 cup/150 g), optional

4 garlic cloves, minced (about 1 tablespoon), optional

2 teaspoons minced ginger

1 green chili, finely chopped

½ teaspoon ground turmeric

1 plum tomato, diced (about ½ cup/110 g)

¾ teaspoon salt, or to taste

1 teaspoon garam masālā (see page 232)

TADKĀ

2 teaspoons neutral oil

Pinch of asafetida, optional

1 teaspoon cumin seeds

½ teaspoon ground red chili (paprika, for mild, or Indian red chili, for spicy), or to taste

Juice of ½ lime (1 to 2 teaspoons), or to taste

2 tablespoons roughly chopped cilantro

1 Place the dāl in a fine-mesh sieve and rinse under running water for about 30 seconds, swishing the dāl around with your fingers to clean it well (see Prep Tip 1). Drain, transfer to a large bowl, and cover with plenty of warm water to soak. Set aside.

2 To cook in a pressure cooker, follow instructions in Prep Tip 2.

3 To cook on the stovetop, heat the oil in a saucepan or pot over medium-high heat. Add the onion (if using) and cook until it starts to caramelize, about 5 minutes, to get some browning. The onion will continue to cook with the dāl.

4 Add the garlic (if using), ginger, and green chili, and cook for about 1 minute. Add 1 tablespoon of water, as needed, if the aromatics begin to burn or stick to the pan. Stir in the turmeric, then add the diced tomato and salt. Cook, stirring frequently, until the tomatoes start to soften, about 1 minute.

5 Drain the soaked dāl and add it and 3 cups (720 ml) water to the saucepan. Bring to a boil, reduce the heat to medium-low, and simmer, uncovered, stirring occasionally (see Prep Tip 3), until the dāl is completely tender, about 30 minutes. Add ½ to 1 cup (120 to 240 ml) water, as needed, if the dāl becomes too thick.

6 Stir in the garam masālā and remove from the heat.

7 To prepare the tadkā, heat the oil in a small pan over medium-high heat. Add the asafetida (if using) and cumin seeds and heat until the cumin seeds begin to brown, 30 to 60 seconds. Remove from the heat, swirl in the red chili, and pour over the hot dāl.

8 Stir in the lime juice and additional salt to taste. Garnish with cilantro, if desired.

VARIATIONS

1   For dāl with greens, stir in about 3 cups (150 to 200 g) packed greens (such as spinach or kale) once the dāl has cooked.

2   For added depth of flavor, add ½ teaspoon black mustard seeds with the cumin and 10 fresh curry leaves with the ground red chili when making the tadkā.

PREP TIP

1   If using chanā dāl or toor/tuver dāl, soak 1 cup (about 200 g) of either dāl overnight in room temperature water and increase the cook time to about 1 hour on the stovetop and 10 minutes in the electric pressure cooker.

2   To cook this dāl in an electric pressure cooker, use the sauté setting to heat the oil at the beginning of step 3, then cook the onion, tomato, and aromatics as specified in steps 3 and 4. Add the dāl and 3 cups (720 ml) water, cover, and pressure cook on high for 5 minutes. Wait for 10 minutes before manually releasing the pressure. Turn on the sauté setting again after pressure cooking, adjust the amount of water to the desired consistency, stir in the garam masālā, and proceed with the tadkā in step 7.

3   This process (unlike with the other dāl recipes in this chapter) involves cooking the dāl with the tomatoes and aromatics. The acid from the tomatoes increases the dāl's cooking time, but in this recipe, slowing down the cooking time just a bit allows the flavors to come together and to replicate that "tastes better the next day" vibe.

Gujarāti Dāl

SERVES 4 TO 6

Characteristically tangy, sweet, and a bit spicy, this dāl, made with tuver/toor dāl (split pigeon peas) is one I grew up on, and it will always remain a staple in our home. Not only is cinnamon traditional in dāl recipes like this, but it also makes it even healthier, since cinnamon consumption is associated with regulating blood sugar levels.[27] Cinnamon and cloves provide a pleasing warmth, and peanuts add a welcome contrast to the smooth dāl. Serve with rice or on its own.

PREP TIME 5 MINUTES
COOK TIME 45 MINUTES

½ cup (100 g) tuver/toor dāl (split pigeon peas; see Prep Tip)

1 tablespoon neutral oil, such as sunflower

¾ teaspoon black mustard seeds

1 cinnamon stick (3 inches/7.5 cm)

1 star anise, optional

2 teaspoons grated ginger

14 to 16 fresh curry leaves, optional but recommended

1 plum tomato, diced (about ½ cup/110 g)

1 teaspoon ground coriander

1 teaspoon ground cumin

½ teaspoon ground red chili

½ teaspoon ground turmeric

4 cloves, ground in a mortar (about ⅛ teaspoon)

1 to 2 tablespoons jaggery or desired sweetener

3 tablespoons raw peanuts, optional

2 pieces of kokum (see page 13), optional

¾ teaspoon salt

1 tablespoon fresh lime juice, to taste

2 tablespoons roughly chopped cilantro, optional

1 Place the dāl in a fine-mesh sieve and rinse under running water for about 30 seconds, swishing the dāl around with your fingers to clean it well. Cook it with 2 cups (480 ml) water in an electric pressure cooker on high for 8 minutes. Wait for 10 minutes before manually releasing the pressure. Alternatively, cook on the stovetop in a large saucepan with 3 cups (720 ml) water, bring to a boil, reduce the heat to medium-low, and simmer, stirring occasionally, until the dāl is fully tender and falling apart, about 1 hour. Blend the cooked dāl until smooth and set aside.

2 Heat the oil in a large saucepan or pot over medium heat until glossy. Add the mustard seeds and heat until they crackle, about 30 seconds. Add the cinnamon stick, star anise (if using), ginger, and curry leaves (if using), and stir for about 30 seconds, then add the diced tomato, coriander, cumin, red chili, turmeric, and cloves and stir to combine.

3 Cook over medium heat, stirring frequently, until the tomatoes have broken down and reduced slightly, about 4 minutes. Add water, 1 tablespoon at a time, if the mixture starts to stick to the bottom of the pot.

4 Add the cooked dāl to the pot and stir well to combine. Add 1 cup (240 ml) water, the jaggery, peanuts (if using), kokum (if using), and salt. Bring to a boil, reduce the heat to medium-low, and simmer to let the flavors develop, about 20 minutes. Stir occasionally and add water as needed to achieve a soupy consistency.

5 Remove the pot from the heat, stir in the lime juice, and adjust the salt, sweetener, and red chili to taste. Add the cilantro (if using), stir well, and serve hot.

PREP TIP Tuver/toor dāl (split pigeon peas) can be soaked for a few hours (or up to a day) to shorten the cooking time. Simply rinse and drain the dry dāl, place in a large bowl, and cover with plenty of cool water. Leave at room temperature, then drain just prior to cooking with water as specified in step 1.

Sāmbār

SERVES 4

Sāmbār is a tangy, spicy South Indian preparation of tuver/toor dāl (split pigeon peas). It has a nutty quality from the use of sāmbār podi (see page 235). Sāmbār is delicious with rice and even better with piping hot Crispy Masala Dosā Rolls (page 32). Tamarind concentrate, available at Indian grocers in small jars, gives this dāl its characteristic tang, but, if unavailable, lime juice may be used to substitute. I use moringa (drumsticks)—also available at Indian grocery stores—but sāmbār can be made with a wide array of vegetables, such as radish, pearl onions, carrots, peas, or eggplant. If you can find fresh or frozen moringa at your local Indian grocer, this is absolutely the recipe for them.

PREP TIME 5 MINUTES
COOK TIME 40 MINUTES

½ cup (105 g) tuver/toor dāl (split pigeon peas)

4 ounces (115 g) frozen, cut moringa (drumsticks)

1 plum tomato, diced (about ½ cup/110 g)

1½ tablespoons sāmbār podi (see page 235; see Ingredient Tip)

½ to 1 teaspoon ground red chili

1 teaspoon salt

2 teaspoons neutral oil, such as sunflower or avocado

Pinch of asafetida, optional

¾ teaspoon black mustard seeds

2 garlic cloves, thinly sliced, optional

10 curry leaves, torn

2 to 3 teaspoons tamarind concentrate, or lime juice

1　Place the dāl in a fine-mesh sieve and rinse under running water for about 30 seconds, swishing the dāl around with your fingers to clean it well. Drain the dāl, then cook it with 2 cups (480 ml) water in an electric pressure cooker on high for 10 minutes. Wait for 10 minutes before manually releasing the pressure.

2　To cook on the stovetop, put the dāl and 3 cups (720 ml) water in a large saucepan. Simmer over medium-low heat, stirring occasionally, until the dāl is fully tender and falling apart, about 1 hour. Using a whisk, mash the cooked dāl until mostly smooth and set aside.

3　In a saucepan, combine the moringa and diced tomato with ½ to 1 cup (120 to 240 ml) water (enough to cover). Boil until starting to become tender, about 5 minutes.

4　Add the dāl along with the sāmbār podi, red chili, and salt, and simmer until it starts to thicken, 10 minutes.

5　Heat the oil in a small pan over medium heat. Add the asafetida and mustard seeds and heat until the seeds begin to pop, about 30 seconds. Reduce the heat to medium-low, add garlic (if using), and stir until lightly browned, about 30 seconds. Remove from the heat and stir in the curry leaves.

6　Add the tempered spices and oil to the sāmbār and continue to simmer for about 5 minutes, adding up to ½ cup (120 ml) water to achieve the desired consistency. Stir in the tamarind concentrate and adjust the salt and chili to taste. Serve hot.

INGREDIENT TIP Store-bought sāmbār podi/masālā often contains red chili and salt, so, if using, omit these two ingredients, reduce the quantity of store-bought sāmbār masālā to 2 teaspoons, and adjust to taste.

Whole Moong Dāl

SERVES 2 TO 4

This dāl is made from hearty whole green moong (called mag in Gujarāti and mung beans around the world), which is rich in fiber and protein. It's a typical dāl you'd expect to find in many Gujarāti households; I learned this variation from my mom. The flavor is similar to Gujarāti Dāl (page 113) because it uses similar spices, but moong itself gives a flavorsome bite and added nuttiness. I recommend using an electric pressure cooker to save time, but this dāl may also be made on the stovetop. Serve with rice or your preferred grain.

PREP TIME 5 MINUTES
COOK TIME 40 MINUTES

½ cup (110 g) whole moong dāl

1 tablespoon neutral oil, such as sunflower or avocado

1 teaspoon cumin seeds

1 teaspoon black mustard seeds

Pinch of asafetida

1 teaspoon minced ginger

2 garlic cloves, minced

10 fresh curry leaves

1 plum tomato, diced

1 teaspoon ground coriander

1 teaspoon ground cumin

½ teaspoon ground turmeric

½ teaspoon ground red chili

1 small cinnamon stick (3 inches/7.5 cm)

4 cloves, ground in a mortar (⅛ teaspoon)

1 tablespoon jaggery (or desired sweetener), or to taste

½ teaspoon salt, plus more to taste

Juice of ½ lime (2 to 3 teaspoons), or to taste

2 tablespoons chopped cilantro

1   Place the dāl in a fine-mesh sieve and rinse under running water for about 30 seconds, swishing the dāl around with your fingers to clean it well. Cook the dāl with 2 cups (480 ml) water in an electric pressure cooker on high for 10 minutes. Wait for 10 minutes before manually releasing the pressure.

2   To cook on the stovetop, soak the moong in plenty of cool water overnight, drain, then place in a saucepan with 3 cups (720 ml) water. Bring to a boil, reduce the heat to simmer, and cook until very tender, stirring occasionally, for about 1 hour.

3   Heat a medium pot or saucepan over medium-high heat. Add the oil and heat until it glides across the pot, about 1 minute. Add the cumin seeds and mustard seeds and swirl the pan until the mustard seeds pop and sizzle, about 30 seconds.

4   Lower the heat to medium. Add the asafetida, ginger, garlic, and curry leaves, and cook until fragrant, about 30 seconds.

5   Add the tomato with a pinch of salt, and cook until softened, 2 to 3 minutes. Add the coriander, cumin, turmeric, chili, cinnamon stick, and cloves and stir to open the flavors, about 30 seconds.

6   Add the dāl with its cooking liquid and 1 cup (240 ml) water to the pot. Stir in the jaggery and salt, and simmer over medium-low heat until the liquid has reduced slightly, about 15 minutes. Add water as needed to maintain a soupy consistency.

7   Remove from the heat and stir in the lime juice and cilantro. Taste and adjust the salt, lime juice, and jaggery. Serve piping hot.

VARIATION Khāttā (tangy) mag: A tangy version of this dāl, and a specialty of my bā (paternal grandmother), made with yogurt for tanginess. Omit the tomato in step 5. Stir in ¼ to ½ cup (60 to 120 g) plain nondairy yogurt (see page 223) in step 7, and finish with lime or lemon juice to taste. This dish works particularly well with Meyer lemon, if available.

Dāl Makhani

SERVES 4 TO 6

Makhani refers to the buttery quality of this dāl, which you'll find more often in Indian restaurants than in home kitchens, due to its richness. The restaurant version is often slow cooked for many hours, but this one, although the cook time is shorter, yields similarly delicious results. It begins with a combination of whole urad, also known as black matpe bean or black gram, and kidney beans, which are cooked until very tender. This variety of dāl tends to cook unevenly, so I recommend adding a small amount of baking soda to ensure even cooking (I tested both with and without, and baking soda truly makes a big difference). The starches from the well-cooked dāl contribute to its creamy texture, which is later enhanced by cashew cream (see Tip for a nut-free alternative). I use nutritional yeast to amplify the buttery flavors, keeping this dish completely dairy-free. Black cardamom and smoked paprika give this dish its classic smoky notes.

⅔ cup (135 g) whole black
   urad dāl

⅓ cup (60 g) dried kidney beans
   or ½ cup (30 g) canned beans,
   drained

1 cinnamon stick
   (3 inches/7.5 cm)

1 bay leaf

1 black cardamom pod

¼ teaspoon baking soda

⅓ cup (50 g) cashews, soaked in
   hot water for 15 minutes

1 tablespoon vegan butter or
   olive oil

1 teaspoon cumin seeds

1 red or yellow onion or 1 fennel
   bulb, finely chopped
   (about 2 cups/300 g)

1 plum tomato, diced

3 tablespoons tomato paste
   (double concentrated, if
   possible)

4 garlic cloves, minced
   (about 1½ tablespoons)

1 tablespoon grated or minced
   ginger

1 teaspoon ground coriander

1 teaspoon ground cumin

½ teaspoon smoked paprika,
   optional

½ teaspoon ground turmeric

¼ teaspoon ground red chili,
   plus more to taste

1 teaspoon salt

2 tablespoons nutritional yeast
   (see page 15), optional

2 teaspoons dried fenugreek
   (kasoori methi), crushed with
   your hands

2 teaspoons garam masālā
   (see page 232)

2 tablespoons roughly chopped
   cilantro

1   Rinse and soak the urad dāl and dried kidney beans in plenty of cool water and leave at room temperature for 8 hours or overnight. If using canned kidney beans, add them in step 6.

2   Combine the soaked dāl and kidney beans with the cinnamon stick, bay leaf, cardamom pod, baking soda, and 3 cups (720 ml) water in an electric pressure cooker and cook on high for 25 minutes. Wait for 10 minutes before manually releasing the pressure. Alternatively, place all the ingredients and 4 cups (960 ml) water in a large pot, bring to a boil, reduce the heat to medium-low, and simmer until very tender, stirring occasionally, for 1 to 1½ hours. (The exact cooking time will vary depending on the brand and age of the dāl.)

3   While the dāl cooks, drain cashews and put in a blender with ⅓ cup (80 ml) water. Blend until smooth and set aside.

4   In a separate large pot or Dutch oven, heat the butter over medium-high heat. Add the cumin seeds and cook until lightly browned, about 30 seconds. Add the onion with a generous pinch of salt and cook, stirring frequently, until it starts to soften, 5 minutes. Lower the heat to medium and continue to cook until the onions have fully softened and begun to caramelize, about 5 minutes.

5   Reduce the heat to medium-low. Add the diced tomato, tomato paste, garlic, ginger, coriander, cumin, paprika (if using), turmeric, red chili, and salt, and cook for 30 seconds.

6   Add ½ cup (120 ml) water and the canned kidney beans (if using), Increase the heat to medium-high and cook, stirring occasionally, until the mixture thickens and the oil begins to separate, about 10 minutes. Remove and discard the bay leaf, cardamom pod, and cinnamon stick.

7   Add the dāl, nutritional yeast (if using), dried fenugreek, cashew cream (reserve about 1 tablespoon for serving), and 1 cup (240 ml) water. Simmer over medium-low heat, stirring occasionally, for 15 minutes. Stir in the garam masālā and add water for the desired consistency. Adjust the salt and red chili to taste. Top with cilantro and serve.

VARIATION   For a nut-free variation, substitute 1 to 1½ cups (240 to 360 ml) plain oat milk or preferred nondairy milk for the cashew cream and water in step 7.

Gujarāti Kadhi

SERVES 4

This sweet and tangy yogurt-based stew is perfect for any chilly day. It is creamy and luxurious and gains brightness from the cilantro and lime juice that finish the dish. Besan or chickpea flour is used here as a thickening agent. This Gujarāti Kadhi, with its added sweetness and slightly thin consistency, is best paired with plain rice or Khichadi (see page 140).

PREP TIME 5 MINUTES
COOK TIME 20 MINUTES

⅔ cup (160 g) unsweetened plain nondairy yogurt (see page 223)

3 tablespoons besan or chickpea flour

1 tablespoon cane sugar

2 tablespoons nutritional yeast (see page 15), optional

1 teaspoon salt

1 tablespoon vegan butter or olive oil

½ teaspoon black mustard seeds

½ teaspoon cumin seeds

¼ teaspoon fenugreek seeds

3 cloves

1 cinnamon stick (3 inches/7.5 cm)

1 bay leaf

2 teaspoons minced ginger

1 green chili, minced

10 curry leaves

Pinch of asafetida, optional

2 tablespoons roughly chopped cilantro

Juice of ½ lime (about 2 teaspoons), optional (depending on the sourness of the yogurt)

1 Whisk together the yogurt, besan, sugar, nutritional yeast (if using), salt, and 2 cups (480 ml) water in a bowl. Set aside.

2 Heat the butter in a large saucepan over medium-high heat, add the mustard seeds, cumin seeds, fenugreek seeds, cloves, cinnamon stick, and bay leaf, and cook until the mustard seeds begin to pop, about 1 minute. Remove from the heat and stir in the ginger, green chili, curry leaves, and asafetida (if using). The mixture will spatter quite a bit.

3 Add 1 cup (240 ml) water, return to the stove, lower the heat to medium, and simmer for about 5 minutes to extract as much flavor as possible from the spices and aromatics.

4 Whisk in the yogurt mixture, increase the heat to medium-high until it simmers, and reduce the heat to medium-low. Simmer until thickened, whisking occasionally, for about 10 minutes. Add more water if needed or simmer it longer until you've reached the desired consistency.

5 Remove from the heat; discard the cinnamon stick, bay leaf, and cloves. Stir in the cilantro and lime juice (if using), and adjust the salt, sugar, and lime to taste.

Rasam

SERVES 2

Rasam derives from the Sanskrit word "rasa," meaning essence. This classic South Indian broth, also known as sāru or chāru, extracts the essence of the spices and other ingredients into a tangy broth that is delicious with basmati rice or simply sipped and savored on its own. It can be made from a wide variety of ingredients, and I've used the classic flavors of black pepper, tomato, and tamarind here. Tamarind concentrate, available in small jars at Indian grocers, can vary in tartness, so it's important to start with a small amount and adjust to taste (see page 15 for more info). If unavailable, lime juice or lemon juice may be added instead, just before serving. Serve this dish on its own or with plain rice.

PREP TIME 5 MINUTES
COOK TIME 10 MINUTES

1 teaspoon coriander seeds

½ teaspoon cumin seeds

¼ teaspoon black peppercorns

¼ teaspoon fenugreek seeds

¼ teaspoon ground turmeric

¼ teaspoon ground red chili

⅓ cup (88 g) cooked tuver/toor dāl (split pigeon peas), optional (see Prep Tip)

1 plum tomato, diced

2 to 3 garlic cloves, smashed

1 tablespoon tamarind concentrate, to taste

¾ teaspoon salt

2 teaspoons neutral oil, such as avocado

Pinch of asafetida

½ teaspoon black mustard seeds

10 to 12 fresh curry leaves

1 to 2 tablespoons chopped cilantro

1 Toast the coriander, cumin, peppercorns, and fenugreek in a dry saucepan over medium heat until fragrant and lightly browned, 5 minutes, then transfer to a small bowl to cool. Using a mortar and pestle or spice grinder, crush the spices to a coarse powder. Mix in the ground turmeric and red chili and set aside.

2 In a large saucepan, place the dāl (if using), tomato, garlic, tamarind, salt, ground spices, and 3 cups (720 ml) water. Bring to a boil, then remove from the heat.

3 Heat the oil in a small saucepan over medium-high. Add the asafetida and mustard seeds. When the seeds begin to spatter, about 30 seconds, add the curry leaves and stir for a few seconds. Pour the mixture over the rasam in the large saucepan and stir well to combine.

4 Adjust the salt, red chili, and tamarind to taste. Top with cilantro and serve piping hot.

PREP TIP The cooked tuver/toor dāl helps thicken the rasam slightly. I reserve some of the cooked dāl when making Gujarāti Dāl or Sāmbār (page 113 or page 114) to use for this purpose. Alternatively, you can toast 2 to 3 tablespoons of dried toor/tuver dāl in a dry pan until lightly browned, about 5 minutes. Then grind in a coffee grinder and add along with the spices. In a pinch, feel free to omit.

BHĀT
Rice Dishes

Rice, one of the grains used most universally throughout Indian cuisine, is the focus of this chapter. Rice, produced across India and exported all over the world, goes hand in hand with a piping hot bowl of Gujarāti Dāl (page 113) or Gujarāti Kadhi (page 121), and it's a star of Butternut Squash and Mushroom Biryāni (see page 134), a complex layered rice dish. I've also included quinoa, which, while not commonly used in India, has been adopted by many Indian American families. Technically a seed that comes from South America, quinoa is delicious with Indian food, and is also a nutritional powerhouse, containing fiber, protein, vitamins, and minerals.

Rice & Quinoa

The plain or spice-infused rice and quinoa varieties here can be served alongside dāls and gravies. My preferred method for cooking rice and quinoa (both of which work well with Indian cuisine) is in my electric pressure cooker, my Instant Pot. This method produces consistent results. Alternatively, feel free to cook the rice/quinoa using your own preferred method—on the stovetop or in a rice cooker according to the package's and/or manufacturer's instructions. Most of the recipes in this chapter begin with precooked rice so that you can easily make the rice ahead of time.

   Whole spices may be used to flavor rice or quinoa while cooking. When I'm serving rice with a gravy dish (see pages 88 to 105), I generally use some combination of these spices: 1 cinnamon stick, 1 bay leaf, 2 to 3 green cardamom pods, 2 to 3 cloves, ½ teaspoon cumin seeds, and a pinch of saffron.

WHITE BĀSMATI RICE

MAKES ABOUT 3 CUPS (385 G)
COOK TIME 15 MINUTES

1 cup (about 185 g) white bāsmati rice (or similar medium to long grain rice, such as jasmine or sonā masuri)

1 Place the rice in a fine-mesh sieve, running cool tap water over it while simultaneously swishing the grains between your fingers. Rinse until the water begins to run clear, then drain the rice.

2 Place the rice and 1 cup (240 ml) water in an electric pressure cooker and cook on high pressure for 4 minutes. Wait for 10 minutes before manually releasing the pressure.

BROWN BĀSMATI RICE

MAKES ABOUT 3 CUPS (400 G)
COOK TIME 30 MINUTES

1 cup (about 175 g) brown bāsmati rice (or similar medium to long whole grain rice, such as jasmine, red, or Sonā Masuri)

1 Place the rice in a fine-mesh sieve, running cool tap water over it while simultaneously swishing the grains between your fingers. Rinse until the water begins to run clear, then drain the rice.

2 Place the rice and 1 cup plus 2 tablespoons (270 ml) water in an electric pressure cooker and cook on high pressure for 18 minutes. Wait for 10 minutes before manually releasing the pressure.

QUINOA

MAKES ABOUT 4 CUPS (525 G)
COOK TIME 12 MINUTES

1 cup (about 180 g) quinoa (any color)

1 Place the quinoa in a fine-mesh sieve, running cool tap water over it while simultaneously swishing the seeds between your fingers. Rinse until the water begins to run clear, then drain the quinoa.

2 Place the quinoa and 1½ cups (360 ml) water in an electric pressure cooker and cook on high pressure for 1 minute. Wait for 10 minutes before manually releasing the pressure.

BROWN
BĀSMATI

QUINOA

WHITE
BĀSMATI

Mint Pea Rice

SERVES 4 TO 6

The combination of mint and peas is very reminiscent of spring, and I use it here to bring brightness to the table any time of year. This recipe works particularly well with leftover cooked rice, since the stir-frying makes it easy to prepare.

PREP TIME 5 MINUTES
COOK TIME 10 MINUTES

¼ cup (about 10 g) packed fresh mint leaves

1 cup (about 50 g) packed baby spinach leaves

1 tablespoon extra virgin olive oil

½ teaspoon cumin seeds

½ teaspoon fennel seeds

⅛ teaspoon asafetida, optional

¾ cup (100 g) frozen peas, thawed

2 teaspoons ground coriander

½ teaspoon ground turmeric

½ teaspoon salt, or to taste

3 cups (about 400 g) cooked white or brown bāsmati rice (see page 126)

Juice of ½ lime (about 2 teaspoons)

Freshly chopped mint, optional

1   Blend the mint and spinach with ½ cup (120 ml) water and set aside.

2   Heat the oil in a wide pan over medium heat. Add the cumin seeds, fennel seeds, and asafetida (if using), and toast until lightly browned and fragrant, about 1 minute.

3   Lower the heat slightly, stir in the peas, and cook until heated through, about 2 minutes. Stir in the coriander, turmeric, and salt, and toast for a few seconds, then add the blended mint and spinach. Cook until slightly reduced, 2 minutes.

4   Add the rice and stir until well combined and heated through, about 2 minutes. Stir in the lime juice, and adjust the salt and lime juice to taste. Garnish with freshly chopped mint (if using).

Navratan Rice

SERVES 4 TO 6

Navratan means "nine gems" and refers to the nine ingredients typically added to a gravy dish of the same name (see Navratan Kormā, page 98). They are a combination of vegetables, nuts, and dried fruit, and you can easily adapt this recipe with gems of your choosing. I've adapted the flavors to create a stir-fried rice dish. It stands up on its own and is a great alternative to a biryāni, a deeply fragrant but labor-intensive layered rice dish (see page 134).

PREP TIME 20 TO 30 MINUTES
COOK TIME 15 MINUTES

Pinch of saffron, optional

1 tablespoon neutral oil, such as sunflower

½ teaspoon cumin seeds

1 carrot, diced (about ⅓ cup/50 g)

½ medium red bell pepper, diced (about ⅓ cup/50 g)

¼ cup (40 g) corn, fresh or frozen and thawed

¼ cup (35 g) frozen peas, thawed

¾ teaspoon salt, plus more to taste

2 garlic cloves, minced (about 1½ teaspoons)

2 teaspoons grated ginger

2 tablespoons roughly chopped cashews

1 tablespoon roughly chopped almonds

1 tablespoon roughly chopped pistachios

1 Medjool date, pitted and finely chopped

1 tablespoon golden raisins

2 teaspoons ground coriander

½ teaspoon ground red chili

½ teaspoon garam masālā (see page 232)

¼ teaspoon ground turmeric

3 cups (about 400 g) cooked white or brown rice (see page 126)

Juice of ½ lime (about 2 teaspoons)

Freshly chopped cilantro and/or mint

Pomegranate arils, optional

1   Combine the saffron (if using) with 2 tablespoons hot water in a small bowl and set aside.

2   Heat the oil in a large, wide pan over medium heat. Stir in the cumin seeds and toast them until they start to brown, about 1 minute.

3   Increase the heat to medium-high, and add the carrot, pepper, corn, peas, and salt. Continue to cook until the vegetables are tender and start to brown, about 5 minutes. Lower the heat if they begin to brown too quickly.

4   Lower the heat to medium. Stir in the garlic and ginger, and cook until fragrant, 1 to 2 minutes. Stir in the cashews, almonds, pistachios, dates, raisins, coriander, red chili, garam masālā, and turmeric, and cook until well combined, 1 to 2 minutes.

5   Add the rice and saffron water, and stir well to combine. Adjust the salt to taste, squeeze in the lime juice, and top with cilantro and pomegranate (if using) before serving.

NOTE   Other food gems to use include chickpeas, black-eyed peas, diced tofu (stir-fried until lightly browned between steps 2 and 3), finely chopped cauliflower (cooked with the other vegetables in step 3), dried cranberries, and dried apricots.

Butternut Squash and Mushroom Biryāni

SERVES 6 TO 8

Biryāni is a fragrant layered rice dish of Persian and Moghul origin that is frequently made with meat. This soul-warming autumnal version (a crown jewel of this cookbook) has seared mushrooms and roasted butternut squash. Caramelized onions play a key role in developing the layers of flavor in a good biryāni, and I use a combination of fennel and onion, which further heightens the seasonal flavors. Time is an important ingredient, too, as each component is treated with care and is individually seasoned to deepen its flavor. I recommend making this dish for special occasions, when you're able to dedicate time to enjoy the process of making it. Use the longest grain bāsmati rice you can find—this dish really relies on its delicate flavor and texture.

PREP TIME 30 MINUTES
COOK TIME 2 HOURS

SAFFRON MILK

¼ cup (60 ml) unsweetened nondairy milk (such as oat or soy)

½ teaspoon saffron

1 teaspoon rose water or kewrā water, optional

RICE

1½ cups (300 g) white bāsmati rice or biryāni rice

1 black cardamom pod, optional

4 green cardamom pods

1 to 2 small pieces mace, optional

1 bay leaf

1 cinnamon stick (3 inches/7.5 cm)

3 cloves

2 teaspoons salt

BUTTERNUT SQUASH

1 small butternut squash, peeled and cut into 1-inch/2.5 cm pieces (about 2 cups/300 g)

1 teaspoon neutral oil, such as sunflower

¼ teaspoon salt

¼ teaspoon fresh garam masālā (see page 232)

MUSHROOMS

2 teaspoons neutral oil

8 ounces (230 g) cremini mushrooms or desired variety, sliced ¼-inch/6 mm thick (about 3 cups)

¼ teaspoon fresh garam masālā (see page 232)

¼ teaspoon salt

MASĀLĀ

1 tablespoon neutral oil

1 teaspoon cumin seeds

½ teaspoon fennel seeds, optional

1 fennel bulb, thinly sliced (about 2 cups/200 g), optional

2 yellow onions, thinly sliced (about 4 cups/600 g)

½ teaspoon salt

6 garlic cloves, minced (about 1½ tablespoons)

1 tablespoon grated ginger

2 teaspoons ground coriander

2 teaspoons ground cumin

1 teaspoon fresh garam masālā (see page 232)

½ teaspoon ground turmeric

½ teaspoon ground red chili, plus more to taste

¾ cup (180 g) unsweetened plain nondairy yogurt (see page 223)

3 tablespoons roughly chopped cilantro

3 tablespoons roughly chopped mint

Freshly chopped fennel fronds

Freshly chopped cilantro and/or mint

Chopped roasted cashews, optional

1   Preheat the oven to 425°F (220°C). Line a large baking sheet with parchment paper.

2   To make the saffron milk, pour the milk into a small saucepan and bring to a boil. Stir in the saffron threads, then remove it from the heat. Stir in the rose water (if using), and set aside.

3   To parboil the rice, put the rice in a fine-mesh sieve, running cool tap water over it while simultaneously swishing the grains between your fingers. Rinse until the water begins to run clear, then drain the rice. Place the rice and 9 cups (2 L) water in a large saucepan and add the cardamom, mace (if using), bay leaf, cinnamon, cloves, and salt. Bring to a boil, reduce to a simmer, and continue to cook until the rice is about three quarters cooked, 5 to 8 minutes. Taste at 6 minutes to check that it's not overcooked (it will finish cooking in the oven). Drain the rice and spices. Set aside.

4   Prepare the butternut squash. Toss the squash with oil and salt and spread the pieces in an even layer on the baking sheet so the pieces are not touching, to ensure that they caramelize. Roast for about 30 minutes, until starting to brown. Remove them from the oven, sprinkle on the garam masālā, and set aside. Adjust salt to taste.

5   While the butternut squash is roasting, prepare the mushrooms. Heat a wide pan over medium-high heat. Heat the oil until glossy, 30 seconds, then add the mushrooms. Sauté until they start to brown, about 5 minutes. Stir in the garam masālā and season with salt to taste. Transfer the mushrooms to a bowl and set aside. Reduce the oven temperature to 375°F (190°C).

6   To make the masālā, heat the oil in the same pan used to sauté the mushrooms. Add the cumin and fennel seeds (if using), and stir until they start to brown, 1 to 2 minutes. Lower the heat to medium, add the fennel (if using) and onion, sprinkle with salt, and cook, stirring occasionally, until the vegetables start to caramelize, about 20 minutes. Add the garlic and ginger and cook until fragrant, about 2 minutes. Stir in the coriander, cumin, garam masālā, turmeric, and red chili, and heat until lightly toasted, about 30 seconds. Remove from the heat and stir in the yogurt, butternut squash, mushrooms, cilantro, and mint. Taste and adjust the salt and red chili. Be sure to season the mixture generously because it will be layered between the rice, which is neutral in flavor.

7   In a 12-inch (30 cm) round baking dish or Dutch oven with a tight-fitting lid, evenly layer the prepared ingredients from bottom to top: one third of the rice and whole cooking spices, 1 tablespoon saffron milk, two thirds of the vegetables, the second third of the rice, the second tablespoon saffron milk, the last third of the vegetables, the last third of the rice, and the last tablespoon of saffron milk.

8   Cover with the lid and bake for 30 minutes or until fully heated through. If the lid isn't tight-fitting, wrap some foil between the lid and the dish to prevent any steam from escaping. Remove the lid, top with fennel fronds, cilantro, and cashews (if using), and serve hot.

Coconut Brown Rice

SERVES 4

Coconut rice is a classic rice dish from South India that is hearty, earthy, and nutty. This version calls for brown rice, which pairs very well with the toasty flavors of coconut and dāl. Frozen grated coconut is readily available at Indian grocers and is quite convenient. Use fresh, if available, for its delicious taste. Dried coconut may be used but is less ideal, and sweetened coconut is too sweet for this recipe.

PREP TIME 15 MINUTES
COOK TIME 5 MINUTES

1 tablespoon neutral oil, such as avocado

1 tablespoon chanā dāl, soaked in hot water for 15 minutes and drained

2 teaspoons split white urad dāl

1 teaspoon black mustard seeds

1 to 2 dried red chilies

¼ teaspoon asafetida

10 curry leaves

¼ cup (40 g) unsalted raw or roasted cashews, optional but recommended

½ cup (70 g) finely grated coconut, fresh or frozen

3 cups (400 g) cooked brown bāsmati rice (see page 126)

¼ to ½ teaspoon salt

1   Heat the oil in a wide pan over medium heat. Add the chanā dāl and urad dāl, and toast until they start to turn light brown, about 1 minute. Stir in the mustard seeds and red chilies, and continue to cook until the mustard seeds start to crackle, about 30 seconds.

2   Lower the heat to medium-low and add the asafetida, curry leaves, cashews (if using), and grated coconut. Stir until toasty and fragrant, about 2 minutes.

3   Add the rice and continue to stir until fully heated through and well combined, 2 minutes. Add water, 1 tablespoon at a time, if the rice becomes too dry. Season with salt to taste.

Lemon Rice

SERVES 4 TO 6

Similar in technique to coconut rice, lemon rice is another classic South Indian rice dish that is both nutty from the peanuts and crunchy dāl and tangy from the lemon. My first memories of lemon rice are of enjoying it as a child at our local Hindu temple, where many of the South Indian volunteers would bring it to serve. This variation is based on the traditional method and inspired by those flavor memories. It tastes best with white rice, but brown works, too!

PREP TIME 15 MINUTES
COOK TIME 15 MINUTES

¼ cup (40 g) peanuts (see Ingredient Tip)

1 tablespoon neutral oil, such as sunflower

1 tablespoon chanā dāl, soaked in hot water for 15 minutes and drained

1 tablespoon split white urad dāl

1 teaspoon black mustard seeds

1 to 2 dried red chilies

A generous pinch of asafetida

¾ teaspoon ground turmeric

12 fresh curry leaves

3 cups (385 g) cooked white bāsmati rice (see page 126)

1 teaspoon freshly grated lemon zest

½ teaspoon salt

1 to 2 tablespoons fresh lemon juice

Freshly chopped cilantro, optional

1 Put the peanuts in a wide pan and toast them dry over medium-low until toasted, about 8 minutes, tossing frequently to prevent burning. Remove them from the pan and set aside.

2 Heat the oil in the pan over medium heat. Add the chanā dāl and urad dāl, and toast them until they start to turn light brown, about 1 minute.

3 Stir in the mustard seeds, red chilies, and asafetida, and heat until the mustard seeds start to crackle, about 30 seconds.

4 Lower the heat to medium-low, swirl in the turmeric, and add the curry leaves. Stir until the curry leaves start to crisp, about 2 minutes.

5 Add the rice, lemon zest, and peanuts, and continue to stir until fully heated through and well combined, 2 minutes. Season with salt and lemon juice to taste.

6 Serve with chopped cilantro (if using) sprinkled on top.

INGREDIENT TIP Skin-on, unroasted peanuts are traditionally used and are available at Indian grocers. Their flavor is slightly more neutral, but if unavailable, use roasted peanuts.

Khichadi

SERVES 4 TO 6

Khichadi is a nourishing and comforting rice and legume porridge enjoyed throughout India. In its simplest form, khichadi is nothing more than bāsmati rice and split yellow mung dāl cooked together with a bit of turmeric. This is often fed to babies as their first solid food (and was fed both to me and my son!). This dressed-up version uses warm spices, such as cinnamon and cloves, and red and green chilies for heat. In lieu of ghee (clarified butter), which is often used, I recommend a combination of olive oil and nutritional yeast. They give this recipe a similar richness and depth of flavor. Khichadi pairs perfectly with chhās (see page 193) or Gujarāti Kadhi (page 121) or simply a dollop of unsweetened plain nondairy yogurt (see page 223). Serve with Indian pickle and crisp pāpad, if desired.

PREP TIME 5 MINUTES
COOK TIME 30 MINUTES

½ cup (100 g) white bāsmati rice

½ cup (110 g) split yellow or split green mung dāl

1 tablespoon olive oil

1 teaspoon cumin seeds

Pinch of asafetida, optional

1 to 2 dried red chilies, optional

1 cinnamon stick (3 inches/7.5 cm)

1 bay leaf

3 cloves

12 to 15 fresh curry leaves, torn, optional

1 green chili, minced

2 teaspoons minced ginger

1 tablespoon nutritional yeast (see page 15), optional

½ teaspoon ground turmeric

½ teaspoon salt

Freshly chopped cilantro, optional

Fresh lime juice, optional

1 Put the rice and dāl in a fine-meshed sieve and rinse under running water until the water runs clear. Drain and set aside.

2 In a deep, wide pot or Dutch oven with a tight-fitting lid, heat the oil over medium-high heat until glossy, 30 seconds Add the cumin seeds and toast until they just start to brown, about 1 minute. Stir in the asafetida (if using), red chilies (if using), cinnamon stick, bay leaf, and cloves, and remove from the heat. Stir in the curry leaves (if using), green chili, and ginger, and mix until well combined and fragrant, about 30 seconds.

3 Add the rice and dāl, 4 cups (960 ml) water, nutritional yeast (if using), turmeric, and salt, and stir well to combine. Bring to a boil, then reduce to a gentle simmer. Cover and continue to simmer until fully tender, 20 minutes. To ensure even cooking, avoid opening the lid, but it's okay to check the water level once or twice (given the quantity of water, it's highly unlikely that the khichadi will stick to the bottom).

4 Remove the lid, increase the heat to medium-high, and stir frequently and gently until the khichadi is slightly thickened to a porridge-like consistency, 3 to 5 minutes. Remove from the heat and adjust the salt to taste.

5 Serve topped with cilantro and lime juice, if desired.

Vegetable Khichadi

SERVES 6

This is a khichadi that my mom would often make for us while we were growing up. She'd always include plenty of veggies to make the dish more substantial, and we never minded eating such a hearty and comforting meal. The love that goes into a pot of khichadi always makes it taste better. What I like about it most is that everything cooks together, making this an easy one-pot meal. Serve with the typical khichadi accompaniments (see page 140) or with a dollop of unsweetened plain nondairy yogurt (see page 223).

PREP TIME 10 MINUTES
COOK TIME 30 MINUTES

½ cup (100 g) white bāsmati rice

½ cup (110 g) split yellow or split green mung dāl

1 tablespoon olive oil

1 teaspoon cumin seeds

Pinch of asafetida

2 bay leaves

1 cinnamon stick (3 inches/7.5 cm)

3 cloves

½ to 1 dried red chili, seeded, optional

12 to 15 curry leaves, torn

1 green chili, minced

1 tablespoon minced ginger

1 teaspoon ground turmeric

½ teaspoon freshly cracked black pepper

3 cups (300 g) roughly chopped cabbage (from ½ small head)

1 russet or large red potato, diced into ½-inch (13 mm) pieces (about 1¼ cups/200 g)

1 carrot, diced (about ½ cup/75 g)

⅓ cup (about 35 g) frozen peas

⅓ cup (about 25 g) corn kernels, fresh or frozen and thawed

2 tablespoons nutritional yeast (see page 15), optional

1 teaspoon salt, plus more to taste

Freshly chopped cilantro, optional

Fresh lime juice, optional

1 Put the rice and dāl in a fine-mesh sieve and rinse under running water until the water runs clear. Drain and set aside.

2 In a deep, wide pot or Dutch oven with a tight-fitting lid, heat the oil over medium-high heat until glossy, 30 seconds. Add the cumin seeds and asafetida and heat until they just start to brown, about 1 minute.

3 Stir in the bay leaves, cinnamon stick, cloves, and dried red chili (if using), and remove from the heat. Stir in the curry leaves, green chili, ginger, turmeric, and black pepper, and mix until well combined and fragrant, about 30 seconds.

4 Add the cabbage, potato, carrot, peas, corn, and a pinch of salt to the pot, return the pot to medium heat, and continue to cook, stirring frequently, until the cabbage begins to soften, about 5 minutes. Add about ¼ cup (60 ml) water during this step if the spices and vegetables start to stick to the bottom of the pot.

5 Add the rice and dāl, 5 cups (1 L plus 180 ml) water, the nutritional yeast (if using), and salt. Bring to a boil, then reduce the heat to medium-low to maintain a gentle simmer. Stir well, then cover, and continue to simmer until the rice and dāl are fully cooked and the vegetables are tender, 20 minutes. To ensure even cooking, avoid opening the lid, but it's okay to check the water level once or twice (given the quantity of water used, it's highly unlikely that the khichadi will stick to the bottom).

6 Remove the lid, increase the heat to medium-high, and stir frequently and gently until the khichadi is slightly thickened to a porridge-like consistency, 3 to 5 minutes. Remove from the heat and adjust the salt to taste.

7 Serve topped with cilantro and lime juice, if desired.

VARIATION Vegetables such as green beans, cauliflower, and bell pepper may be used in place of any of the vegetables in this recipe.

UNCOOKED HEARTY
MASĀLĀ KHICHADI

Hearty Masālā Khichadi

SERVES 6

Different combinations of legumes, grains, and seeds may be used to make khichadi. The heartiness in this version comes from the combination of brown rice, whole mung dāl, quinoa, and tuver/toor dāl (split pigeon peas), all packed with fiber and well-balanced plant protein. This recipe is perfectly suited for electric pressure cookers, since brown rice and whole mung dāl take much longer to cook on the stovetop. Serve with any khichadi accompaniments (see page 140).

PREP TIME 5 MINUTES
COOK TIME 40 MINUTES

½ cup (90 g) brown bāsmati rice

½ cup (105 g) whole moong dāl

½ cup (100 g) tuver/toor dāl (split pigeon peas)

½ cup (90 g) quinoa

1 tablespoon olive oil

1 teaspoon cumin seeds

1 yellow onion, diced (about 2 cups/300 g)

Salt

4 garlic cloves, minced

1 tablespoon minced ginger

1½ teaspoons ground coriander

1½ teaspoons ground cumin

1 teaspoon ground red chili

1 teaspoon garam masālā (see page 232)

½ teaspoon ground turmeric

Freshly chopped cilantro

1 Put the rice, moong dāl, tuver dāl, and quinoa in a fine-mesh sieve and rinse under running water until the water runs clear. Drain and set aside.

2 Set the electric pressure cooker to high sauté mode. Add the oil, heat for a few seconds, then add the cumin seeds and toast them until they start to brown, about 30 seconds. Add the onion and a pinch of salt, and continue to sauté until the onions start to turn translucent, about 5 minutes. Stir in the garlic and ginger and continue to cook until fragrant, 1 to 2 minutes. Add the coriander, cumin, red chili, garam masālā, and turmeric and stir for a few seconds. Quickly add 4 cups (1 L) of water. Turn off the sauté mode.

3 Stir in the rice-dāl-quinoa mixture and 1 teaspoon salt. Cover and pressure cook on high for 18 minutes. Wait 10 minutes before manually releasing the pressure.

4 Serve garnished with freshly chopped cilantro.

Vaghārelā Quinoa

SERVES 4 TO 6

Although quinoa has been used for centuries in South America, it wasn't immediately popular in our family until the early 2000s, when, like many other Indian Americans, my bā and my mom found it worked particularly well with Indian flavors. This Gujarāti-style vaghārelā (stir-fried) quinoa is a tribute to them. It's simpler in flavor than the other rice dishes in this chapter, so it's a good side dish with dāl (see pages 110 to 119) or Gujarāti Kadhi (page 121).

PREP TIME 15 MINUTES
COOK TIME 5 MINUTES

1 tablespoon olive oil

¾ teaspoon cumin seeds

¾ teaspoon black mustard seeds

Pinch of asafetida

10 fresh curry leaves

2 teaspoons grated ginger

4 cups (525 g) cooked quinoa (see page 126)

½ teaspoon ground turmeric

¼ to ½ teaspoon ground red chili

½ teaspoon salt

Fresh lime juice

1   Heat the oil in a wide pan over medium-high heat until shimmering, 30 seconds. Add the cumin seeds, mustard seeds, and asafetida, and heat until the mustard seeds begin to spatter, 30 seconds. Remove from the heat and stir in the curry leaves and ginger until fragrant, about 30 seconds.

2   Return the pan to medium heat and stir in the cooked quinoa and the turmeric, red chili, and salt. Stir until well combined and heated through, about 3 minutes. Remove from the heat.

3   Serve with lime juice squeezed on top.

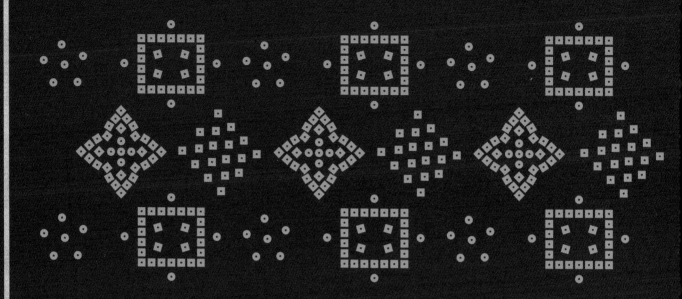

ROTLI
Indian
Flatbreads

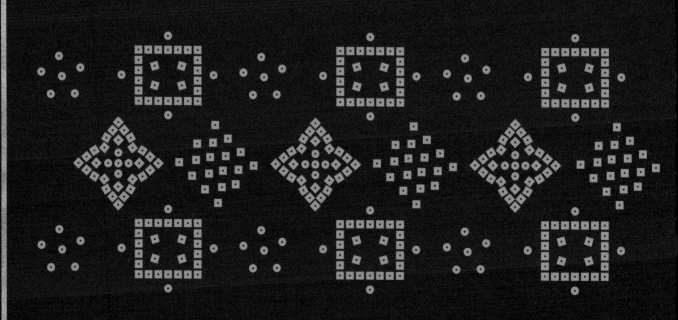

The world of Indian breads is vast, with numerous varieties throughout the country. Here I present some of the most common Indian flatbreads (with less common but more unique variations). They can be served alongside any of the vegetable and/or lentil dishes in this book. Before making any of these breads, read the first recipe for rotli (the quintessential Indian flatbread and therefore the namesake of this chapter) on page 155. I use it as a foundational recipe for making the rest of the breads. You'll find general tips and recommendations that will make the process more approachable.

A NOTE ON GLUTEN-FREE BREADS

Most of the recipes in this book are gluten-free, but those in this chapter are not, because the bread recipes I've featured rely heavily on wheat flours. I understand and respect the need for some to avoid gluten. There are several traditionally gluten-free Indian breads, such as bājri nā rotlā (made from millet) and makki ki roti (made from corn). However, it was a conscious decision to omit gluten-free breads here, since I claim no authority or expertise in making them. Gluten-free flours are widely available, and I've even seen gluten-free roti/chapāti blends at my local Indian grocery. Those would be a good place to start if you'd like to attempt making these bread recipes gluten-free. See page 40 for pudlā, a gluten-free alternative to flatbread that's made from chickpea flour.

Rotli

MAKES 8 ROTLI

Rotli (a Gujarāti word), also known in other Indian languages as roti, chapāti, and phulkā, is probably the most widely made Indian flatbread. It begins with whole wheat flour (see Note 1). Rotli are characteristically thin, soft, and pliable so that they may be used to scoop up vegetable dishes such as Rasāvāla Baby Potatoes (page 84) and Flāvar Vatānā Nu Shāk (page 68). This is a daily bread, best made at home, where the heart is. Enjoy making rotli—the process can even be meditative!

Each rotli-maker has their own method. My mom's and my mother-in-law's methods are my inspiration. Two master rotli-makers, they've made rotli on a weekly basis (if not daily) since they were children. If you're new to Indian flatbreads, I suggest mastering this one first before trying the others. Don't worry if your first attempt isn't perfect. After you've made rotli once, you'll start to get the hang of it: how the dough should feel between your palms, how much salt to use, and how long to cook it. Give it another try or two, and you'll get there! Note 3 will show you the kitchen utensils you'll need to prepare this recipe and every other bread recipe in this chapter. I've made the instructions as clear as possible for beginners. If you're a seasoned Indian home cook, I hope this recipe helps you teach the next generation of rotli-makers!

PREP TIME 5 MINUTES
COOK TIME 1 HOUR

1 cup (125 g) āttā (whole wheat flour), plus more for rolling

½ teaspoon salt

1 teaspoon neutral oil, such as avocado or sunflower (see Note 2)

1 to 2 tablespoons vegan butter or additional neutral oil, optional

1   Clear away space on your countertop for rolling, ideally near the stove. Line an 8-inch (20 cm) diameter steel or plastic container with a lid (or a rotli or tortilla warmer) with a small piece of paper towel or a small tea towel to keep the rotli warm.

2   Fill a wide bowl with extra āttā (about ¼ cup/30 g) and keep it nearby. Have ready a 10-inch (20 cm) nonstick or cast-iron tavā (flat skillet) as well as a metal grate or cooling rack, if you're using an electric stove.

3   In a large mixing bowl, mix 1 cup (125 g) āttā and the salt together with your fingers. Drizzle the oil over the flour and continue to mix to form a sandy texture.

4   Add about ½ cup (120 ml) hot (not boiling) water to a bowl or cup with a spout. Pour ¼ cup (60 ml) of the water evenly over the flour and begin to combine with your dominant hand. Keep your other hand clean to add additional water as needed.

5   Continue to add water, 1 to 2 teaspoons at a time, while mixing, to form a soft and slightly sticky dough (see Note 4).

6   Knead the dough with your knuckles for 1 to 2 minutes, until the dough feels evenly moist. Add more flour if the dough becomes too wet, or sprinkle in some more water if the dough feels too dry. The goal is a dough that is as moist as possible but not enough to stick to the bowl.

7 Form the dough into a ball and coat it with a thin layer of oil. Place it into the mixing bowl and cover with a plate or damp kitchen towel. Set aside to rest for 20 to 30 minutes.

8 Remove the dough from the bowl, knead for a few seconds, then divide into 8 equal portions using a kitchen scale if you have one (although you'll be hard-pressed to find a traditional Indian household that does this). Roll each piece of dough into a ball and flatten slightly. Working quickly, place the balls of dough back into the bowl, and cover to prevent them from drying out.

9 Preheat the skillet over medium heat. Roll out the first rotli by dipping both sides of the dough into the bowl of āttā.

10 Place the dough in the center of your work surface and begin to roll with a rolling pin, applying gentle pressure and letting your elbows do most of the work. Lift and rotate the dough about 90 degrees every few rolls to ensure an evenly round shape. Dust more āttā as needed when lifting, to prevent the rotli from sticking to the work surface.

11 Continue rolling into a thin, 5 to 6-inch (12 to 15 cm) diameter circle. Dust off any excess flour and place onto the preheated skillet.

12 Cook until small bubbles begin to form and the dough starts to turn slightly opaque, 30 seconds. Using tongs, flip the rotli and cook for about 20 seconds, to just barely start cooking the other side.

13 If using an electric stove, move the skillet aside and replace with a kitchen grate. Working quickly, transfer the rotli onto the grate. It should start to puff, and to assist it, gently press with the tongs. Cook for 10 seconds, flip, and cook for another 10 seconds, until some darker spots appear (see Notes 5 and 6).

14 If using a gas stove, transfer the rotli directly from the skillet to the burner grate and follow the same process as in step 13.

15 Place the rotli into the prepared container, spread a thin layer of butter (if using) on top, and quickly cover the container loosely with its lid. You'll place the next rotli directly on top.

16 Repeat the steps for the remaining rotli (see Note 7).

17 Rotli are best served fresh and warm, but they can also be stored at room temperature in an airtight container for about two days. To reheat, simply place on a skillet over medium heat, a few seconds on each side, until warmed through.

NOTES

1 Āttā, also known as chapāti flour or chakki āttā, is available at Indian grocers or online. Āttā is made from finely milled Indian durum wheat, which differs slightly in texture, flavor, and gluten content from all-purpose or whole wheat flours in the West. This difference is key but not critical, and if unavailable, a combination of ½ cup (60 g) all-purpose flour and ½ cup (60 g) whole wheat pastry flour works fine. Another alternative is multigrain "āttā" (made from a blend of wheat, sorghum, millet, and sometimes other flours), also available at Indian grocers, which yields wonderful rotli since it is specifically made for this purpose. If you're new to the process, I recommend using a kitchen scale to measure the flour, but this isn't completely necessary.

2 Oil is optional when making rotli. My mom makes hers without, and they're always perfect in texture. I find that, for beginners, a small amount of oil helps ensure that your rotli remain soft.

3 Rolling directly onto a clean countertop will work fine but, if possible, use a pātlo. This is a wooden or steel rolling board available at Indian grocers or online. Set a kitchen towel underneath to keep it stable. You'll also need a rolling pin and kitchen tongs; the rolling pin I use is a velan, which is a thin dowel-like rolling pin that is thicker at the center. For tongs, I use chipyo, which are thin and flat tongs, but any type of either tool will do.

4 The exact amount of water will vary depending on the brand of flour used, and the humidity and temperature in your kitchen, as well as other factors. I generally use ¼ cup plus 2 to 3 tablespoons (85 to 95 ml) water, depending on the thirst of my āttā that day.

5 A common beginner's mistake is for the rotli to become hard or crisp instead of soft and pliable. To troubleshoot: First, you may need to use more water when kneading your dough. Second, you may need to let the dough rest longer. Third (this is the most common), you may need to cook your rotli for a shorter time or at a lower temperature. Err on the side of undercooking rotli. (However, a hard/crisp rotli is not a bad one! That's what my dad prefers.) Fourth, be sure to stack the rotli and cover while preparing more, to prevent them from drying out.

6 If your rotli aren't puffing evenly, press on the puffed areas to encourage the dough to puff further in other areas. This may be due to the rotli not being evenly rolled out. Regardless, rotli that are not fully puffed will turn out just fine in the end!

7 An experienced rotli-maker can roll out the next one at 30-second intervals, but this is certainly not the goal. I don't recommend pre-rolling all of the rotli at the same time since they can dry out. It's easiest to have a helper either to roll or to cook the rotli, but the rotli-making process can certainly be a one-person job.

VARIATIONS Rotli dough can also be made with pureed vegetables or greens, which add loads of color and nutrients. Below are rough quantities and suggestions to get you started, but once you've mastered the basic technique, the options are endless!

Blend your choice of vegetable with 2 to 3 tablespoons water. Use this purée in place of the water in step 4 to make the dough. Add additional water as specified in step 5 to form a smooth and soft dough. The exact amount of water will vary depending on the vegetable.

Here are color options.

Red: ½ roasted red bell pepper

Deep red/purple: ½ steamed or boiled red beet

Orange: ½ roasted orange bell pepper or 1 steamed or boiled carrot

Yellow: ½ roasted yellow bell pepper plus ¼ teaspoon ground turmeric

Green: about 1 cup (50 g) greens of choice (such as kale or spinach), blanched or steamed, with excess water squeezed out

Parāthā

MAKES 8 PARĀTHĀ

Parāthā is another common homemade flatbread. This recipe begins the same way as Rotli (page 155); the key difference is that it's cooked with oil, which makes it slightly chewier. This recipe can produce two different versions, one simple and one more layered and flaky. The technique for the flaky one is similar to a laminated pastry dough. Parāthā pairs well with vegetable dishes, such as Butternut Squash Chanā Nu Shāk (page 71), but it also works particularly well with gravy dishes, such as Chhole (page 94).

PREP TIME 5 MINUTES
COOK TIME 1 HOUR

1 cup (125 g) āttā, plus more for rolling (see Ingredient Tip)

½ teaspoon salt

1 teaspoon neutral oil, such as avocado or sunflower, plus more as needed

1 Follow steps 1 through 9 for making rotli dough (pages 155 to 156), and be sure to incorporate the oil into the dough.

2 Place an āttā-coated ball of dough in the center of your work surface and roll into a 4 to 5-inch (10 to 12 cm) circle, lifting and rotating about 90 degrees every few rolls to ensure an evenly round shape. Dust with more flour as needed when lifting, to prevent the parāthā from sticking to the work surface. To make unlayered parāthā, continue to roll into a 6-inch (15 cm) circle and proceed with step 4.

3 To make layered parāthā, spread or brush a thin, even layer of oil (about ¼ teaspoon) onto the rolled dough. Sprinkle on a thin layer of āttā (about ½ teaspoon) with your fingers, then fold the dough in half. Repeat the process of layering oil and sprinkling flour, then fold in half again to form a triangle. Roll out the dough gently, flouring as needed, to form a larger triangle about 5 to 6 inches (12 to 15 cm) on each side.

4 Heat a medium nonstick or cast-iron skillet over medium heat. Place the parāthā on the skillet and cook until the dough starts to become opaque, about 30 seconds. Flip over and cook until light brown spots begin to form on the bottom, about 30 seconds.

5 Spread a thin layer of oil (about ¼ teaspoon) onto the top of the parāthā, then flip it and spread another layer of oil onto the other side. Gently press the parāthā with the back of a spatula to cook the bottom until evenly browned, 10 to 20 seconds. Flip over one last time and cook until evenly browned on the other side, 10 to 20 seconds.

6 Transfer the parāthā to a container lined with a paper towel or clean tea towel and cover loosely. Repeat with the remaining dough, placing new parāthā on top of the finished ones.

7 Parāthā are best served hot, but leftovers will stay fresh in an airtight container for up to 3 days.

VARIATIONS

1 Like rotli, parāthā can be made with pureed vegetables in the dough (see page 157).

2 Parāthā can be made with mashed ripe avocado, blended silken tofu, or plain nondairy milk, which create a softer texture. Add ¼ cup of your choice when blending the dough together, and adjust the amount of water to create a smooth dough.

INGREDIENT TIP

Add ½ teaspoon carom seeds, cumin seeds, or chia seeds to the flour when making the dough for added flavor and texture.

Gobi Parāthā

MAKES 4 PARĀTHĀ

Gobi parāthā is a simple flatbread stuffed with a spiced cauliflower mixture, and it's one of my favorites. Enjoy this bread warm with a cooling rāitā (see page 224) or Chhundo (page 220). This particular method for stuffing the parāthā comes from my aunt, and I've found it yields the best results, with even filling. And you can use this method to stuff your parāthā with anything you like. The potato mixture from Dābeli Crostini (page 28) or the green pea mixture from Green Pea Kachori Toasts (page 27) are also great fillings. There are restaurants in India dedicated to making dozens of different types of stuffed parāthā, so the options are truly endless once you learn the basics.

PREP TIME 40 MINUTES
COOK TIME 20 MINUTES

1 recipe Rotli dough
  (see page 155), set aside for
  20 to 30 minutes

2 cups (200 g) grated cauliflower,
  about ½ large cauliflower

½ teaspoon salt, plus more to taste

1 teaspoon ground coriander

½ teaspoon ground cumin

½ teaspoon garam masālā
  (page 232)

½ teaspoon grated ginger

½ teaspoon ground red chili

¼ teaspoon āmchur (dried green
  mango powder) or ½ to
  1 teaspoon lime juice

¼ teaspoon carom seeds

āttā, for rolling and dusting

Neutral oil, such as avocado or
  sunflower

1 Combine the cauliflower and salt in a large mixing bowl and set aside for about 15 minutes, to draw out any moisture from the cauliflower. Transfer the cauliflower to a fine-mesh sieve and press with a large spoon to remove as much water as possible. Return the cauliflower to the mixing bowl and combine with the coriander, cumin, garam masālā, ginger, red chili, āmchur, and carom seeds. Adjust the salt and spices to taste.

2 Divide the dough into 8 equal balls, using a kitchen scale if possible. Keep covered.

3 Flatten and roll out 2 dough balls into 4-inch (10 cm) disks, dusting with flour as needed. Place one quarter of the cauliflower filling in the center of the first disk, leaving about ½ inch (13 mm) uncovered around the edge. Sprinkle ¼ to ½ teaspoon flour over the filling and, with wet fingers, moisten the edges of the dough, place the second disk on top, and press around the edges to seal.

4 Dust the top and bottom of the dough with more flour and begin to roll gently into an 8-inch (20 cm) circle with a velan or rolling pin.

5 Heat a medium nonstick or cast-iron skillet over medium heat. Place the parāthā on the skillet and cook until light brown spots begin to form, about 2 minutes.

6 Flip and cook until light brown spots form on the other side, 1 to 2 minutes. Spread or brush a thin layer of oil (about ¼ teaspoon) on top of the parāthā.

7 Flip and cook until the brown spots deepen in color, 1 minute. Brush with oil, flip again, and cook until the brown spots turn darker on the opposite side, about 1 minute.

8 Repeat the process with the remaining parāthā, layering one on top of the other. Serve warm.

Theplā

MAKES 8 THEPLĀ

Theplā is Gujarāt's spiced version of a parāthā. They're also made with methi (fenugreek) leaves, which lend a pleasantly bitter and earthy flavor, but these can just as easily be omitted. I use a small amount of besan as well as nondairy yogurt to give a soft texture. These flatbreads pair perfectly with Chhundo (page 220). They can also be served with vegetable dishes, like Flāvar Vatānā Nu Shāk (page 68).

PREP TIME 40 MINUTES
COOK TIME 30 MINUTES

1 cup (125 g) āttā (see page 157)

¼ cup (36 g) besan or chickpea flour

1 tablespoon white sesame seeds

1 tablespoon cane sugar

1 teaspoon oil, plus more for cooking

½ teaspoon salt

½ cup (35 g) finely chopped fresh fenugreek leaves (methi; see Ingredient Tip)

¼ cup (60 g) unsweetened plain nondairy yogurt (see page 223), at room temperature (see Variation)

2 garlic cloves, finely minced or grated

1 teaspoon grated ginger

½ teaspoon ground coriander

½ teaspoon ground cumin

¼ teaspoon ground red chili

¼ teaspoon ground turmeric

1 Mix the āttā, besan, sesame seeds, sugar, oil, and salt together in a large bowl, using clean fingers to form a sandy texture. Add the fenugreek leaves, yogurt, garlic, ginger, coriander, cumin, red chili, and turmeric, and mix well with your dominant hand, adding hot water with your clean hand, 1 teaspoon at a time (6 to 8 teaspoons), to form a soft dough. Shape into a dough ball, coat with a thin layer of oil, cover, and let rest for about 20 minutes.

2 Divide the dough into 8 equal balls, using a kitchen scale if possible. Keep covered.

3 Begin to roll each theplu (singular for theplā). Flatten a ball of dough, dust with āttā, and place onto a work surface. Roll, applying gentle pressure with a velan or rolling pin, from the center outward, lifting and rotating about 90 degrees every few rolls to ensure an evenly round shape. Dust with more flour as needed when lifting, to prevent the theplu from sticking to the work surface. Oil may also be used instead of āttā, to prevent the theplu from becoming dry.

4 Heat a medium nonstick or cast-iron skillet over medium heat. Place the theplu on the skillet and cook until the dough starts to become opaque, about 30 seconds. Flip and cook until light brown spots begin to form, about 30 seconds.

5 Spread a thin layer of oil (about ¼ teaspoon) on the top of the theplu, then flip it and spread another layer of oil on the other side. Gently press the theplu with the back of a spatula to cook the bottom until evenly browned, 10 to 20 seconds. Flip again and cook until evenly browned, 10 to 20 seconds.

6 Transfer the theplu to a container lined with a paper towel or clean tea towel and cover loosely. Repeat with the remaining dough, placing new theplu on top of the finished ones.

7 Serve warm or at room temperature.

VARIATION Nondairy yogurt may be substituted with an equal volume of plain nondairy milk, mashed avocado, or blended silken tofu. Adjust the amount of water as needed.

INGREDIENT TIP Fresh fenugreek leaves (methi) work best for this recipe, but you can also use an equivalent amount of chopped cilantro or spinach, 1 tablespoon dried fenugreek leaves (kasoori methi), or omit altogether.

Nān

MAKES 8 NĀN

Nān is easily the most widely known Indian bread in the West. Ironically, it's rarely made in Indian households, and it's generally enjoyed when eating out. This is because nān is cooked in a tandoor (clay oven), not in a home oven. Vegan nān is rarer to find since most nān are made with some form of dairy. This recipe is a wonderful alternative to the restaurant classic. Nān begins with a leavened dough made from all-purpose flour, its gluten content yielding perfectly fluffy yet chewy bread. Feel free to experiment with including whole wheat flour in different amounts for a more healthful version, starting with a 1:1 ratio of whole wheat to all-purpose. You can also infuse minced garlic (2 cloves) or ginger (1 teaspoon) into the dough while kneading, or infuse the vegan butter (if using) with herbs, such as mint or curry leaves. Serve with your favorite gravy-style Indian dishes (see pages 88 to 105).

PREP TIME 1 HOUR AND 15 MINUTES
COOK TIME 40 MINUTES

2 cups (250 g) all-purpose flour, plus more as needed

1 tablespoon cane sugar

2¼ teaspoons (7 g) active dry yeast

½ cup (120 g) unsweetened plain nondairy yogurt (see page 223), warmed to room temperature

½ teaspoon salt

1 tablespoon vegan butter, melted, optional

Freshly chopped cilantro, optional

1 Put the all-purpose flour in a large bowl and set aside.

2 In a small bowl, combine the sugar and yeast with ⅓ cup (80 ml) warm water and mix well with a spoon. Set aside until the yeast foams on top, about 10 minutes.

3 Add the yeast mixture, yogurt, and salt to the flour. Stir together until well mixed. Knead the dough in the bowl, adding flour or water 1 tablespoon at a time as needed to form a smooth and soft dough, 2 to 3 minutes. (It will need less kneading than Western bread doughs do.)

4 Place the dough in the large bowl, cover with a damp tea towel, and leave in a warm place (such as the oven with the oven light on) to rise until doubled in size, about 1 hour.

5 Divide the dough into 8 equal pieces.

6 Roll each piece out into a 6-inch (15 cm) circle (or oval), ⅛ to ¼ inch (6 to 13 mm) thick, dusting with flour as needed.

7 Heat a medium nonstick or cast-iron skillet over medium-high heat. Place the nān in the skillet and cook until bubbles begin to form evenly and brown spots start to appear on the bottom, 2 to 3 minutes. Flip it over and cook until browned on the other side, 30 to 60 seconds. Alternatively, flip onto a grate placed over the flame to achieve charring characteristic of a tandoor.

8 Brush the nān with butter, if desired, place onto a serving plate, and repeat with the remaining pieces.

9 Serve the nān piping hot, cut in half or in quarters, if desired, and topped with freshly chopped cilantro (if using).

MITHĀI
Desserts

Indian desserts have a reputation for being overly sweet, time-consuming, and heavily reliant on dairy. This is partly true. For example, gulāb jāmun, a common North Indian dessert, is essentially a deep-fried, dairy-based donut bathed in simple syrup. However, I believe desserts should be indulgent, and I do enjoy a good vegan one from time to time. This chapter contains variations on classic Indian desserts that are simple to prepare, completely dairy-free, less sweet, and just as delicious. Some of the recipes, such as Sheero with Grapes and Basil (page 177) and Fruit Salad (page 181), are inspired by childhood memories, which make them very special to me.

NOTES ON MANGOES

1   Most mangoes you'll find in grocery stores in the US are imported from Mexico and are generally best from April through September. My favorite variety that's readily available where I live is Kent, but any variety will do. The most important thing is that mangoes should be perfectly ripe. I generally purchase firm, slightly green mangoes when possible and allow them to ripen at home. The danger in purchasing ripe mangoes is that there's a chance they quickly overripen and spoil.

2   Ripening mangoes at home takes a bit of patience and care, but the rewards are worth the effort. I like to ripen my mangoes in a cool, dry place, usually in a corner of my kitchen. I check on them daily, using smell and touch as my guides. As mangoes ripen, they will give off a sweet and intoxicating smell and will give just slightly when gently pressed with your thumb. Once this level of ripeness is achieved, it's best to eat them right away or to refrigerate (for up to a week) until ready to use. Judging on color alone can be dangerous as it can lead to overripe mangoes, since a perfectly ripe mango may be more green than yellow or red.

3   I'm extremely biased when I say that Indian mangoes are the best in the world. I've had the great fortune of eating mangoes in India during May and June, the hottest months, when the fruits are truly at their peak. My favorite varieties are Alphonso and Kesar. While it's possible to find mangoes imported from India, it can be difficult and pricey.

4   I don't recommend using frozen mangoes (I never do unless I freeze them myself). Frozen mangoes from the store nearly always disappoint. Frozen Indian mango varieties can be found at Indian grocers and are a worthwhile alternative to fresh if needed. Canned mango pulp is also available, but this is usually artificially colored and sweetened. Some versions are labeled as natural and unsweetened, and while I don't fully believe the labels, they're a feasible alternative to fresh as well.

Keri No Ras

SERVES 1 TO 2

Keri no ras means "essence of mango" in Gujarāti. It's simply a perfectly ripe mango blended until smooth and served as an accompaniment to any Gujarāti meal, sometimes topped with ground toasted cumin. I've provided the simplest recipe to introduce this most prized fruit of Indian cuisine to you.

PREP TIME 5 MINUTES

1 ripe mango
1 tablespoon cumin seeds, optional
Pinch of ground ginger, optional

1 Peel the mango with a sharp paring knife.

2 Score both sides of the mango to the core, first horizontally, then vertically. Make two more cuts and remove the mango flesh from both sides, cutting as close to the pit as possible.

3 Score the remaining two slimmer sides of the mango and cut again to remove the flesh.

4 Scrape off any remaining bits of fruit with the knife. (Eat whatever is left of the mango directly off the pit, known as keri chusvu in Gujarāti.)

5 Place the mango in a blender and blend until smooth. Add water 1 tablespoon at a time (about 2 to 3 tablespoons total) to reach a thinner consistency, similar to a smoothie. Store in a container in the refrigerator until ready to use. Ras is best enjoyed chilled.

6 To prepare the ground toasted cumin (if using), place the cumin seeds in a small pan over medium heat, stirring frequently, until fragrant and deeper brown in color, 3 to 5 minutes. Allow the cumin to cool, then grind with a mortar and pestle or spice grinder into a coarse powder. Top each serving of ras with a pinch of ground cumin and a pinch of ground ginger, if desired.

NOTE If you've allowed your mango to ripen, you should not need to add any sweetener to your ras. Sometimes, though, a pinch of sugar can help bring out the flavors. It is certainly not necessary.

Oat Kheer

SERVES 2

Kheer is a form of rice pudding, but it can also be made with tapioca, rice noodles, or even oats, as it is here. It's creamy, comforting, and floral in flavor from the cardamom, saffron, and rose water. Cardamom is a key delicious flavor, and healthful, too. Cardamom oils (ideally when the pods are freshly ground) have been shown to have powerful anti-inflammatory and anti-cancer properties.[28]

PREP TIME 5 MINUTES
COOK TIME 15 MINUTES

2 cups (480 ml) unsweetened nondairy milk

2 tablespoons maple syrup or desired sweetener, to taste

½ teaspoon freshly ground cardamom

⅛ teaspoon saffron, crushed

Pinch of salt

1 cup (80 g) old-fashioned rolled oats

½ teaspoon rose water, optional

Pistachios, roughly chopped

Dried rose petals

Saffron

Pinch of ground cardamom

1 Put the milk and ½ cup (120 ml) water in a large saucepan and bring to a boil. Stir frequently. Reduce the heat to a simmer and add the maple syrup, cardamom, saffron, and salt. Stir and simmer until slightly reduced, 2 to 3 minutes. Remove ½ cup (120 ml) of the mixture and set aside for serving.

2 Add the rolled oats to the milk and simmer, stirring occasionally, until creamy and tender, 10 to 12 minutes. Remove from the heat and stir in the rose water (if using) just before serving.

3 Serve in two bowls, topped with the reserved milk, pistachios, rose petals, saffron, and cardamom.

Gājjar No Halvo
Baked Oatmeal

SERVES 2 TO 4

Gājjar no halvo, also known as gājjar kā halwā, is a carrot-based dessert made of grated carrots slowly cooked in milk and sugar. Its comforting warmth will soothe you on any cold day. A nutritious dessert that's rich in anti-inflammatory compounds, fiber, and omega-3 fatty acids, this dish beats out even the heartiest breakfasts. Popping everything in the oven makes the process much simpler. Feel free to top with warmed nondairy milk and a drizzle of maple syrup after baking to make the consistency thinner and to sweeten it.

PREP TIME 10 MINUTES
COOK TIME 30 MINUTES

1 cup (100 g) old-fashioned rolled oats

2 tablespoons ground flax seeds

1 tablespoon chia seeds

1½ teaspoons ground cinnamon

½ teaspoon ground ginger

½ teaspoon ground cardamom

Pinch of grated nutmeg

Pinch of salt

1½ cups (360 ml) unsweetened soy milk or preferred nondairy milk

2 ripe bananas, mashed (about ¾ cup/180 g)

2 carrots, grated (about ¾ cup/75 g)

5 Medjool dates, finely chopped (about ½ cup/75 g)

1 teaspoon vanilla extract or vanilla bean paste

⅓ cup (40 g) chopped raw nuts, such as almonds, pistachios, or walnuts

Unsweetened nondairy milk, warmed

Maple syrup

Pinch of ground cinnamon

1 Preheat the oven to 350°F (175°C).

2 Mix together the oats, flax, chia, cinnamon, ginger, cardamom, nutmeg, and salt in a large bowl until well combined.

3 Add the soy milk, bananas, carrots, dates, vanilla, and half of the chopped nuts, and mix until thoroughly combined.

4 Transfer the mixture to an 8 to 9-inch (20 to 23 cm) round, square, or oval baking dish. Sprinkle with the remaining nuts and bake until the oats and carrots are tender, about 30 minutes.

5 Serve warm with a bit of warmed milk, a drizzle of maple syrup, and a pinch of ground cinnamon. Keep leftovers in the refrigerator for a few days and reheat with more milk as needed.

Sheero with Grapes and Basil

SERVES 4 TO 6

One of the ways my parents remained in touch with their culture and religious traditions was by creating a community with other Indian Americans in our neighborhood. They would gather frequently to celebrate Hindu festivals, and sweets and snacks would be on hand, potluck style. My mom would always bring home a plate of these treats for us. One of my favorites was sheero, a classic pudding made from sooji or ravo (cream of wheat or semolina). It would often be topped with a tulsi (holy basil) leaf for its fragrance. Alongside the plate of goodies would always be sliced grapes, which tasted wonderful with the warm sheero in a single bite. In this recipe I've combined creamy sheero with grapes and holy basil leaves. A fruity olive oil perfectly complements these flavors and replaces the large quantity of ghee that is traditionally used in this dish.

PREP TIME 5 MINUTES
COOK TIME 15 MINUTES

2 tablespoons extra virgin olive oil

1 cup (165 g) fine sooji or ravo (cream of wheat or semolina)

⅓ cup (75 g) cane sugar

½ teaspoon freshly ground cardamom

2 cups (480 ml) unsweetened plain nondairy milk (such as soy or oat)

1 cup (150 g) halved grapes, black, red, green, champagne, or a variety

6 holy basil (tulsi) or basil leaves

1 Heat the oil in a wide nonstick pan over medium-high heat. Add the sooji, reduce the heat to medium, and toast until golden brown and fragrant, about 10 minutes. Stir frequently with a heatproof spatula and lower the heat to prevent burning, if needed.

2 Stir in the sugar, cardamom, and milk, and continue to stir continuously until thickened and separating from the pan, about 3 minutes.

3 Serve immediately in a serving bowl, topped with grapes and basil.

Chocolate Chāi Mousse with Berries

SERVES 4 TO 6

This creamy mousse is subtly spiced with chāi flavors. The ground tea leaves give it a slightly astringent and bitter taste that contrasts well with sweet berries. This is best when fresh berries are at their summertime peak. The creaminess comes from silken tofu, available in vacuum-packed containers in the Asian or dairy aisles of many supermarkets. Not only is this dessert delicious, but it's also nutritious! Dark chocolate and berries are rich in antioxidants. Berries have anti-cancer properties, and dark chocolate plays a role in heart health,[29] too.

PREP TIME 20 MINUTES
COOL TIME 4 TO 12 HOURS

1 cup (150 g) 60 to 70 percent dark or semisweet chocolate, chopped

2 tablespoons maple syrup or desired sweetener

2 tablespoons unsweetened nondairy milk (such as oat or soy)

1 to 1½ teaspoons chāi masālā (page 239)

1 teaspoon black tea leaves, optional

12 ounces (340 g) silken tofu, at room temperature and drained

1 teaspoon vanilla extract or vanilla bean paste

Pinch of salt

Fresh berries, such as raspberries, sliced strawberries, blackberries, and blueberries

1 Prepare a double boiler with 2 cups (240 ml) water in a medium saucepan. Bring to a boil and reduce the heat to low, keeping the water at a simmer. Place a steel or heatproof glass bowl on top. Be sure that it does not touch the water.

2 Add the chocolate, maple syrup, milk, chāi masālā, and tea leaves (if using) to the double boiler and stir with a spatula until fully melted, 3 to 5 minutes. Alternatively, in a microwave, melt using 15-second pulses, stirring after each pulse. Be very careful not to scorch the chocolate.

3 Pour the chocolate mixture, tofu, vanilla, and salt into a blender, and blend until very smooth. Adjust the sweetener and chāi masālā to taste.

4 Divide among 4 to 6 small cups, cover, and refrigerate for at least 4 hours or overnight.

5 Serve with fresh berries on top.

Fruit Salad

SERVES 4 TO 6

This fruit salad, also known as fruit custard, differs from the typical American version because there's a sweet vanilla custard that encases the fruits. It's a common Indian American dinner party dessert I enjoyed while growing up. It's simultaneously creamy and refreshing. The fruits here are merely suggestions. Use any of your favorites (see Note 1)!

PREP TIME 45 MINUTES
COOL TIME 8 TO 12 HOURS

3 tablespoons cornstarch (see Note 2)

3 cups (480 ml) unsweetened nondairy milk (such as oat or soy)

2 to 3 tablespoons cane sugar or alternative sweetener to taste

¼ teaspoon freshly ground cardamom

⅛ teaspoon ground turmeric, optional

1 teaspoon vanilla extract

1 medium ripe mango, peeled and diced

½ ripe banana, peeled and diced

¾ cup (120 g) sliced grapes

6 strawberries, quartered

2 mandarin oranges, peeled and separated into segments

½ apple, diced

8 lychees, peeled, pitted, and quartered

¼ cup (40 g) blueberries

1 Place the cornstarch and 3 tablespoons water in a small bowl and whisk together. Set aside.

2 Combine the milk, sugar, cardamom, and turmeric (if using) in a saucepan. Bring to a boil, then reduce the heat to a simmer. Whisk frequently and watch carefully to prevent it from boiling over. Continue to simmer until slightly reduced, about 5 minutes.

3 Whisk in the cornstarch slurry over medium-low heat, stirring constantly, until thickened to a puddinglike consistency, about 5 minutes. Stir in the vanilla. Remove from the heat and set aside. Allow to cool for about 15 minutes.

4 Combine the fruits in a large storage container. Hold a fine-mesh sieve over the container and pour the custard through onto the fruit. Mix well to combine. Cover and refrigerate until fully chilled, about 4 hours or ideally overnight (see Note 3).

NOTES

1 There are limitless options when it comes to fruits that can be used for this dessert. The only requirement in my mind is that you use a large variety! I aim for about 4 cups (650 g) in total. Other fruits that I like are pineapple, chikoo/sapota, and pomegranate.

2 Please do not substitute other thickeners for cornstarch. I tested this recipe with arrowroot starch, and the result was a gooey mess.

3 This resting period will allow the liquid from the fruits to be released, adding to the flavor of the custard. That will also thin the custard to a milkier consistency.

CARDAMOM COFFEE CAKE
AND BLUEBERRY, FENNEL,
AND LEMON CAKE

Cardamom Coffee Cake

MAKES ONE 8-INCH (20 CM) CAKE

This cake is one of the most popular recipes on my website, so I knew it deserved a spot in this book. The sweetness of the cake pairs well with the subtle bitterness of coffee, and the floral touch of cardamom combined with rich brown sugar takes it over the edge! It pairs perfectly with a cup of coffee or chāi.

PREP TIME 10 MINUTES
BAKE TIME 35 MINUTES
COOL TIME 1 HOUR

1½ cups (200 g) all-purpose flour, whole wheat pastry flour, or oat flour

½ cup (110 g) cane sugar

2 tablespoons cornstarch

1 teaspoon baking powder

½ teaspoon baking soda

¼ teaspoon salt

½ cup (120 ml) unsweetened soy milk or preferred nondairy milk

¼ cup (60 ml) unsweetened applesauce

¼ cup (60 ml) neutral oil, such as sunflower, plus more for greasing

1 tablespoon lemon juice

1½ teaspoons vanilla extract

BROWN SUGAR TOPPING

¼ cup (50 g) brown sugar

1 tablespoon all-purpose flour

1 tablespoon instant coffee powder

1 tablespoon neutral oil

1 teaspoon freshly ground cardamom, cinnamon, chāi masālā, or pumpkin pie spice

Pinch of salt

1 Preheat the oven to 350°F (175°C).

2 Combine the flour, sugar, cornstarch, baking powder, baking soda, and salt in a large bowl and set aside.

3 For the brown sugar topping, in a small bowl, combine the brown sugar, flour, coffee powder, oil, and cardamom. Set aside.

4 In a second small bowl, stir together the soy milk, applesauce, oil, lemon juice, vanilla, and ½ cup (120 ml) water. Let rest for a few minutes. The liquid will likely look curdled, and that's fine.

5 Line an 8-inch (20 cm) round metal cake pan with parchment paper and/or grease the bottom and sides of the pan with a small amount of oil.

6 Pour the wet ingredients into the dry ingredients, mixing slowly and gently with a spatula. Don't overmix the batter. It's fine if some small lumps remain.

7 Pour half of the batter into the prepared pan, then sprinkle on half of the brown sugar topping. Pour in the rest of the batter and spread evenly. Sprinkle on the remaining brown sugar topping and swirl a toothpick or chopstick through the batter a few times.

8 Bake the cake for about 35 minutes, until the top is golden brown and an inserted toothpick comes out clean.

9 Let the cake rest for about 5 minutes, then remove from the pan and transfer to a cooling rack for about 1 hour before cutting and serving (see Storage Tip).

STORAGE TIP This cake tastes best when fresh, but it will keep in an airtight container on the counter for one day. You can store it in the fridge, warming it before eating, as it can become dry in the fridge.

NOTES Baking is a science as much as an art, and each ingredient in this recipe plays an important role.

1 Lemon juice and baking soda react to provide leavening, and baking powder adds an extra leavening boost.

2 Applesauce keeps this cake moist and adds a subtle flavor that brings out the natural "fruity" undertones of coffee.

3 Cornstarch lends binding, which is vital for vegan cakes.

4 Soy milk offers the protein structure important in the crumb of the product

For these reasons, I don't offer many substitutions for this recipe.

Blueberry, Fennel, and Lemon Cake

MAKES ONE 8-INCH (20 CM) CAKE

I love blueberries in any form, so much so that our wedding cake was blueberry and lemon flavored. In this cake, their summery flavors are paired with fennel seeds, a common Indian after-dinner breath freshener. Blueberries freeze remarkably well, so this cake can be enjoyed year-round.

PREP TIME 10 MINUTES
BAKE TIME 35 MINUTES
COOL TIME 1 HOUR

1½ cups (180 g) all-purpose flour

¾ cup (165 g) cane sugar

2 tablespoons cornstarch

2 teaspoons freshly ground fennel seeds

1 teaspoon baking powder

½ teaspoon baking soda

¼ teaspoon salt

½ cup (120 ml) unsweetened soy milk or preferred nondairy milk

¼ cup (60 ml) unsweetened applesauce

¼ cup (60 ml) neutral oil, such as sunflower, plus more for greasing

1 tablespoon lemon juice

1 teaspoon lemon zest

1½ teaspoons vanilla extract

2 cups (225 g) blueberries

1 tablespoon all-purpose flour

Raw sugar, optional

1 Preheat the oven to 350°F (175°C).

2 Put the flour, sugar, cornstarch, fennel seeds, baking powder, baking soda, and salt in a large bowl and whisk together. Set aside.

3 In a small bowl, put the milk, applesauce, oil, lemon juice, lemon zest, and vanilla. Add ½ cup (120 ml) water, stir together, and let rest for a few minutes. The liquid will likely look curdled, and that's fine.

4 Line an 8-inch (20 cm) round metal cake pan with parchment paper and/or grease the bottom and sides of the pan with a small amount of oil.

5 Pour the wet mixture into the dry ingredients, mixing slowly and gently with a spatula. Don't overmix the batter; it's fine if some small lumps remain.

6 In a medium bowl, toss the blueberries and the flour together until well coated.

7 Pour half of the batter into the prepared pan and sprinkle on half of the blueberries. Pour in the rest of the batter and spread evenly. Sprinkle on the remaining blueberries. Add a sprinkling of raw sugar if desired.

8 Bake the cake until the top is golden brown and an inserted toothpick comes out clean, 45 to 50 minutes.

9 Let the cake rest for about 5 minutes, then remove from the pan and transfer to a cooling rack for about 1 hour before cutting and serving.

Pecan Nānkhatāi

MAKES 18 TO 20 COOKIES

Nānkhatāi is a crisp biscuit often made from nuts, spices, and a combination of flours, and it's designed to be dunked into piping hot chai. Whole pecans, oats, and nutmeg create a warmth that pairs wonderfully with Masālā Chāi (page 197). Purists won't miss the traditional ghee, either—this version is made with olive oil and the difference is not at all detectable.

PREP TIME 15 MINUTES
BAKE TIME 30 MINUTES
COOL TIME 30 MINUTES

½ cup (60 g) raw pecans

1 cup (100 g) rolled oats

½ cup (60 g) all-purpose flour

1 cup (120 g) powdered sugar

1 teaspoon baking powder

¾ teaspoon freshly grated nutmeg

3 tablespoons extra virgin olive oil

1 tablespoon soy milk

2 teaspoons vanilla extract or vanilla bean paste

Finely chopped pecans, optional

1 Preheat the oven to 350°F (175°C). Line a baking sheet with parchment paper.

2 Put the pecans and oats in a blender and blend until powdery. Pour them into a large bowl and add the flour, sugar, baking powder, and nutmeg.

3 Stir in the oil, soy milk, and vanilla to form a smooth dough. Form balls with 1 tablespoon of dough and place them on the baking sheet about 2 inches (5 cm) apart.

4 Gently flatten each ball and press a pinch of finely chopped pecans into each one, if desired.

5 Bake for 25 to 30 minutes, until golden brown. Remove from the oven, let sit for 5 minutes, and transfer to a cooling rack. Let the cookies cool completely before enjoying.

VARIATION Experiment with other nuts and spices. You can substitute pistachios for pecans and cardamom for nutmeg for a more traditional flavor combination.

PINU
Drinks

A wide array of ingredients, from nuts and seeds to herbs, flowers, and fruits, come together in different combinations in these traditionally inspired Indian beverages. It's certainly a challenge to distill all the delicious beverages that Indian cuisine has to offer into a single chapter. Here, I've covered many of the most popular along with some of my own variations adapted to my Western kitchen. I've organized them by consistency—yogurt-based, milk-based, and water/juice-based. I use soy-, nut-, or oat-based yogurts or milks in place of dairy to remain quite true to the originals. The yogurt drinks (such as Chhās, page 193) are cooling and work well with spicier dishes (such as Hearty Masālā Khichadi, page 146), the milk-based drinks (such as Masālā Chāi, page 197) are warming and comforting, and the water/juice-based ones (such as Orange Curry Leaf Cooler, page 206) are bright and refreshing.

Chhās

SERVES 1

Chhās is a savory, thin, yogurt-based drink particularly popular in Gujarāt. It's a cooling accompaniment to any Indian meal and goes especially well with warm, spicy dishes, such as Vegetable Khichadi (page 143).

PREP TIME 5 MINUTES

¼ cup (60 g) chilled plain unsweetened nondairy yogurt (see page 223)

½ teaspoon chāt masālā (see page 236)

Salt, to taste

1 Whisk together the yogurt, chāt masālā, and ½ cup (120 ml) ice-cold water in a pitcher. Season with salt to taste.

2 Serve immediately, poured into glasses with a small amount of crushed ice, if desired, and topped with cilantro or mint for a touch of freshness. You can also store it in the refrigerator until ready to drink.

Lassi

SERVES 2

Lassi (pronounced "luh-see") is a yogurt-based drink celebrated throughout India, with origins in Punjab and other northern states. As with anything you make in the kitchen, your lassi will only be as good as the ingredients you use. Refer to page 223 for information regarding nondairy yogurt to be sure you use one that is tasty, since the flavor of the yogurt will be prominent in this drink. For mango lassi, use the ripest mango you can find (see page 168). I've offered a few lassi variations here, but you can make it with any seasonal fruits or herbs of your choosing.

PREP TIME 5 MINUTES

½ cup (120 g) unsweetened plain
  nondairy yogurt (see page 223)

Crushed ice, optional

BEET ROSE

1 ripe medium banana, peeled,
  sliced, and frozen

½ medium beet, boiled or
  steamed, and diced

1 tablespoon maple syrup or
  desired sweetener, or to taste

2 teaspoons rose water, plus more
  to taste

BLUEBERRY CARDAMOM

1 cup (120 g) frozen blueberries

1 tablespoon maple syrup or
  desired sweetener, or to taste

⅛ teaspoon freshly ground
  cardamom

MANGO

1 ripe mango, peeled and diced

1 tablespoon maple syrup or
  desired sweetener, or to taste

MINT

1 ripe medium banana, peeled,
  sliced, and frozen

20 fresh mint leaves

1 tablespoon maple syrup or
  desired sweetener, or to taste

½ cup (about 25 g; a generous
  handful) packed fresh spinach
  leaves

Pinch of salt

Combine the yogurt and ingredients of your choosing in a blender with ¼ to ½ cup (60 to 120 ml) ice-cold water. Blend until smooth. Adjust the sweetener to taste and the amount of water to desired consistency. Serve immediately in a glass with a small amount of crushed ice, if desired.

Masālā Chāi

SERVES 2

Masālā Chāi is the classic Indian spiced milk tea made from loose-leaf black tea. I recommend boiling it on the stovetop, as it's an important step in extracting the flavor of both the spices and the tea leaves. However, there is no single correct way to make chāi. Some prefer theirs creamier and others thinner, and some like it spicier and ginger-heavy while others lean toward sweeter and more floral flavors. This recipe reflects my happy medium: creamy and fragrant, on the sweeter side, and not too spicy. Experiment with your own ratios, using this recipe as a starting point (see Note 1).

PREP TIME 15 MINUTES

1 small cinnamon stick
    (1½ inch/4 cm)

4 black peppercorns

8 green cardamom pods

1 teaspoon fennel seeds, optional

2 tablespoons raw sugar

1½ teaspoons grated ginger

1 tablespoon CTC black tea or
    1½ tablespoons loose-leaf black
    tea (see Ingredient Tips)

2 cups (480 ml) plain oat milk,
    unsweetened if possible (see
    Ingredient Tips)

1 Using a mortar and pestle, gently crush the cinnamon, peppercorns, cardamom pods, and fennel seeds (if using), and set aside.

2 In a medium saucepan, combine 1½ cups (360 ml) water and the raw sugar, and bring to a simmer. Add the ginger and crushed spices. Reduce the heat and let simmer gently to fully infuse the spices into the water, about 5 minutes. The water should be caramel in color and extremely fragrant.

3 Add the tea leaves and continue to simmer to steep and deepen in color, about 3 minutes.

4 Pour in the milk and increase the heat to medium-high. Lift a ladleful of chāi a few inches (or a foot, if you're daring), then pour it back into the saucepan a few times. This is a technique used by roadside chāi vendors to aerate the tea and further enhance the flavors.

5 Let the chāi boil to the brim (see Note 2) for 2 to 3 minutes, then remove from the heat. Return to the heat and boil once more to the brim, about 30 seconds. Remove from the heat again, strain into serving glasses or mugs, and enjoy warm.

NOTES

1 Don't feel limited to the spices listed here. Other spices that work well are star anise, nutmeg, mace, and saffron. Add dried rose petals or dried jasmine flowers for a more floral version. Chāi masālā (see page 239), a combination of ground spices, may also be used in place of whole spices. Simply add 1 teaspoon when boiling the water and omit the ginger and whole spices. Adjust the amount of chāi masālā to taste.

2 Don't worry if your chāi doesn't boil to the brim, as there are numerous factors that are involved in making this possible. Boil the chāi after adding the milk, until it turns a deep amber color, 4 to 5 minutes. Your chāi may threaten to boil over, so keep your eye on the pot. But don't worry too much, since boiling over a pot of chāi and cleaning it up is basically a rite of passage into chāi mastery.

INGREDIENT TIPS

1 Any loose-leaf black tea variety will work, such as Darjeeling, Assam, or even Earl Grey. CTC (crush, tear, curl) tea is most traditional, but I recommend reducing the quantity, since it tends to be stronger. Get to know the variety of your choosing and adjust to your desired level of potency.

2 I've found oat milk to be the best plant-based milk for chāi, suitable even for dairy lovers, but use whatever nondairy milk you prefer. I also like unsweetened soy milk (plus it's more nutritious), but it does change the taste slightly in a way that may not appeal to some. I also often use a 1:1 ratio of oat and soy milk to get the best of both worlds in this recipe. I wouldn't recommend using nut-based milks, as they tend to be waterier and often separate in the boiling process.

Mint Lemongrass Chāi

SERVES 2

Making this version of chāi always transports me to Mumbai, where my bā (grandma) would tear homegrown lemongrass from her plant on the windowsill, which perfumed the whole kitchen when boiled. Mint and lemongrass give the chāi an herbaceous brightness that is simply unparalleled.

PREP TIME 15 MINUTES

2 tablespoons raw sugar

3 tablespoons roughly chopped fresh lemongrass (the bottom half of a thin stalk)

2 teaspoons grated ginger

1 tablespoon CTC black tea or 1½ tablespoons loose-leaf black tea (see page 197)

20 fresh mint leaves (1 small handful)

2 cups (480 ml) unsweetened plain nondairy milk (preferably oat, see page 197)

1 In a saucepan, combine the sugar and 1 cup (240 ml) water and bring to a boil. Add the lemongrass and ginger. Reduce the heat to medium-low and simmer gently to fully infuse the spices into the water, about 3 minutes.

2 Add the tea leaves and mint, and continue to simmer for about 3 minutes.

3 Pour in the milk and increase the heat to medium-high. Lift a ladleful of chāi a few inches (or a foot, if you're daring), then pour it back into the saucepan a few times. This is a technique used by roadside chāi vendors to aerate the tea and further enhance the flavors.

4 Let the chāi boil to the brim (see Note) for 2 to 3 minutes, then remove from the heat. Return to the heat and boil once more to the brim, about 30 seconds.

5 Remove from the heat, strain into serving glasses or mugs, and enjoy warm.

NOTE Don't worry if your chāi doesn't boil to the brim, as there are numerous factors that are involved in making this possible. Boil the chāi after adding the milk, until it turns a deep amber color, 4 to 5 minutes. Your chāi may threaten to boil over, so keep your eye on the pot. But don't worry too much, since boiling over a pot of chāi and cleaning it up is basically a rite of passage into chāi mastery.

Hazelnut and Pistachio Thandāi

SERVES 4

Commonly enjoyed during Holi, the springtime Hindu festival of colors, this drink is refreshing as well as nutty, spicy, and sweet. It begins with nuts and seeds that are blended and combined with milk. The hazelnuts complement the subtle flavor of pistachios. Many versions also have cashews, almonds, melon seeds, and white poppy seeds, so feel free to experiment. Fennel seeds are key here, and I add a generous amount. If you prefer a subtler flavor, reduce the amount by half.

PREP TIME 5+ HOURS

6 Medjool dates, pitted
  (about 90 g)

¼ cup (35 g) raw hazelnuts

¼ cup (35 g) raw pistachios

1½ teaspoons fennel seeds

6 green cardamom pods, crushed
  and husks removed

6 black peppercorns

Pinch of saffron

1½ cups (480 ml) unsweetened
  plain nondairy milk
  (preferably soy or oat)

1 to 2 teaspoons rose water

Dried rose petals, optional

1 Place the dates, hazelnuts, pistachios, fennel seeds, cardamom, peppercorns, and saffron in a blender and cover with 1½ cups (480 ml) boiling water. Cover and let soak for about 1 hour. Add the milk and blend until very smooth, then stir in rose water to taste.

2 Transfer the mixture to a pitcher and refrigerate for at least 3 hours (ideally overnight) until completely chilled. If desired, the thandāi can be passed through a fine-mesh sieve or cheesecloth/nut milk bag for a smoother consistency. Serve over ice and garnish with rose petals, if desired.

Haldar Nu Doodh

SERVES 2

Haldar nu doodh is Gujarāti for turmeric milk. It consists of warmed milk and ground turmeric. This humble drink has since gained wide popularity in the West as "golden latte," clearly a more appealing name. I've come to enjoy this version, which uses additional warm spices and a touch of maple syrup to balance the turmeric flavor and create a more well-rounded beverage.

PREP TIME 10 MINUTES

1½ cups (360 ml) plain nondairy milk (preferably soy or oat; see Ingredient Tips)

¼ teaspoon ground cinnamon (see Ingredient Tips)

¼ teaspoon ground ginger

¼ teaspoon ground turmeric

⅛ teaspoon ground black pepper

1 tablespoon maple syrup or desired sweetener, or to taste, optional

1   Combine the milk and ½ cup (120 ml) water in a small saucepan. Whisk in the cinnamon, ginger, turmeric, and black pepper, and bring to a simmer.

2   Reduce the heat to medium-low and simmer gently, whisking occasionally to froth the milk, until slightly thickened, about 5 minutes. Add maple syrup (if using) to taste, and serve warm.

INGREDIENT TIPS

1   Other nondairy milks can be used here. If using a nut-based milk, use 2 cups (480 ml) milk and no added water.

2   If you have chāi masālā (see page 239), feel free to use 1 teaspoon in place of the cinnamon, ginger, and black pepper.

Ginger Lime Sharbat

MAKES ABOUT ⅔ CUP (150 ML) SYRUP, 5 TO 10 SERVINGS

Sharbat, a drink with Persian roots, is a flavored syrup diluted with water, creating a bright and refreshing beverage for any time of the day. Jaggery lends a complex caramelly flavor, but if unavailable, you can substitute your preferred sweetener.

PREP TIME 3 HOURS

Zest of 1 medium lime

¼ cup (60 g) finely chopped jaggery

1 tablespoon grated ginger

1 tablespoon lime juice

¾ to 1 cup (180 to 240 ml) chilled sparkling or still water

Crushed ice

Lime slices or wedges

Mint leaves, optional

1   Combine 1 heaped teaspoon lime zest, the jaggery, ginger, and ½ cup (120 ml) water in a small saucepan and bring to a boil. Simmer over medium-low heat until the jaggery is completely dissolved and the syrup has reduced slightly, 5 minutes. Remove from the heat and let stand for about 15 minutes for the flavors of lime and ginger to fully infuse into the syrup.

2   Strain the syrup into a small glass jar, stir in the lime juice and refrigerate until completely cooled, 2 to 3 hours. It will stay fresh for up to 2 weeks in the refrigerator.

3   When ready to serve, stir together the chilled water with 1 to 2 tablespoons syrup, adjusting to taste. Serve with a small amount of crushed ice, lime slices, and mint leaves (if using).

Orange Curry Leaf Cooler

SERVES 2

Nonalcoholic beverages sometimes have a bad reputation for being unpleasantly sweet and lacking dimension. I'm hoping to disprove this notion with the aromatic blend of herbaceous, spicy, and citrusy flavors that makes this a punchy mocktail to sip and savor. Choose your favorite orange variety from the three suggested.

PREP TIME 1 HOUR

1 navel, Cara Cara, or blood orange

1 small chunk ginger (½ inch x ½ inch/13 mm x 13 mm)

6 fresh curry leaves

2 teaspoons maple syrup or desired sweetener, or to taste

1 cup (150 g) ice cubes

½ to 1 cup (120 to 240 ml) chilled sparkling water

1 Place two serving glasses in the freezer to chill, about 1 hour.

2 Using a paring knife, peel the orange, taking care not to remove any white pith. Roughly chop the peel, set aside, and juice the orange.

3 Put 2 teaspoons chopped orange peel, the ginger, curry leaves, and maple syrup into a cocktail shaker and muddle for approximately 30 seconds. Add ½ cup (120 ml) orange juice and the ice cubes, cover, and shake vigorously for 30 seconds. Pour into the chilled glasses. Serve topped with ¼ to ½ cup (60 to 120 ml) chilled sparkling water per glass.

Iced Lemon Mint Chāi

SERVES 2

This refreshing iced tea was developed with my brother, Shawn, and sister-in-law, Roaya, in mind. Roaya, of Persian heritage, loves all things tea, and Shawn, an avid golfer, is a big fan of the lemonade and iced tea beverage popularized by the professional golfer it's named after. Here's my take on that drink. It's perfect for a hot summer day.

PREP TIME 3+ HOURS

1 medium lemon

4 black peppercorns

4 cloves

4 green cardamom pods

10 to 15 fresh mint leaves (a small handful), plus more if desired

1 tablespoon loose-leaf black tea

1 to 2 tablespoons maple syrup or desired sweetener, to taste

1 Zest the lemon, taking care not to remove any white pith. Set the zest aside and chill the lemon in the refrigerator until ready to serve.

2 Gently crush the black peppercorns, cloves, and cardamom pods using a mortar and pestle or spice grinder. Put the crushed spices and 3 cups (720 ml) water in a saucepan and bring to a boil. Reduce the heat to medium and boil gently to fully infuse the flavors in the water, 10 minutes. Remove from the heat, stir in the lemon zest, mint leaves, and tea. Steep for 5 to 7 minutes, depending the strength desired.

3 Strain the tea into a heatproof pitcher. Cover the pitcher and refrigerate until fully chilled, at least 3 hours and up to 2 days.

4 When ready to serve, cut the lemon in half, juice half into a small bowl, and thinly slice the other half. Remove the chāi from the refrigerator and stir in the maple syrup and 2 to 3 teaspoons lemon juice, adjusting both to taste.

5 Serve over ice in tall glasses and garnish with lemon slices and mint leaves, if desired.

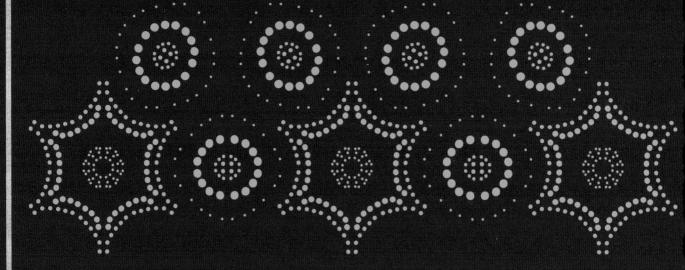

CHUTNEY
AND OTHER
CONDIMENTS

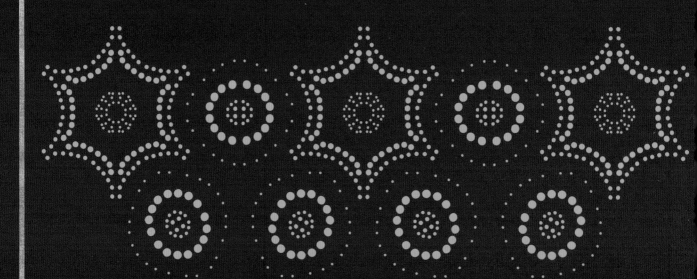

C hutney has established its popularity throughout India and abroad. There are hundreds, if not thousands, of variations of this illustrious condiment. Nearly every chutney begins with a base of herbs (e.g., cilantro or mint) or fruit (e.g., dates or tamarind), sometimes a thickening agent such as nuts, spiciness (any combination of spices, chili, garlic, and ginger), acid (from the fruit base, āmchur/dried green mango powder, or lime), and salt (often kālā namak/black salt for depth of flavor). The word "chutney" is probably more aptly spelled "chatni" to keep with the spelling conventions of this book, but I've intentionally used the most common spelling here since it's more easily recognized.

In this chapter are the essential chutneys, the classics such as green and coconut. And I've included recipes for nondairy yogurt and other condiments, such as Mint Cucumber Rāitā (yogurt-based, page 224) and Chhundo (mango-based, page 220). You'll find plenty of serving suggestions, but don't feel limited. I hope you'll discover many ways to create your own variations and uses for chutney.

Green Chutney

Green chutney is an essential accompaniment to many Indian meals, and here you'll find two versions. Mint Cilantro Chutney pairs wonderfully with Tofu Tikkā (page 23), and Cilantro Peanut Chutney is essentially made for Kale and Broccoli Pudlā (page 40). I leave the green chili variety up to you; Thai green chili is spicier, and seeded jalapeño is milder. Choose the one that pleases your palate, but don't omit it altogether. And don't feel limited by the greens or nuts listed here. Variations with other herbs, such as basil, and other nuts, such as pistachios or walnuts, would be wonderful.

MINT CILANTRO CHUTNEY

MAKES ABOUT 1 CUP (200 G)
PREP TIME 10 MINUTES

2 cups (100 g) packed, roughly chopped cilantro, including stems

¼ cup (20 g) packed, roughly chopped mint leaves

¼ cup (38 g) unsalted cashews, raw or roasted

1 tablespoon minced ginger

1 green chili, or to taste

½ teaspoon ground cumin

½ teaspoon āmchur (dried green mango powder), optional but recommended

½ teaspoon black salt, or to taste

2 teaspoons fresh lime juice (½ lime), or to taste

CILANTRO PEANUT CHUTNEY

MAKES ABOUT 1 CUP (200 G)
PREP TIME 10 MINUTES

2 cups (100 g) packed, roughly chopped cilantro, including stems

¼ cup (40 g) unsalted peanuts, roasted or raw

2 teaspoons minced ginger

1 garlic clove

1 green chili, or to taste

1 tablespoon fresh lime juice (½ lime), or to taste

1 Medjool date, pitted

½ teaspoon ground cumin

¾ teaspoon black salt, or to taste

Place all of the ingredients in a blender along with ¼ cup (60 ml) water. Blend and add more water as needed to achieve desired consistency. Adjust the heat (chili), salt, and acid (lime) to taste. Serve immediately or refrigerate in an airtight container for up to a few days. Squeeze a bit of lime juice or place a thin slice of lime on top to preserve the chutney's vibrant green color.

NOTE It's best to slightly over-season chutney since it's not meant to be eaten alone. Āmchur (dried green mango powder) and black salt (kālā namak) are used here to give a lip-smacking piquancy and a pleasantly funky saltiness. If needed, more lime juice may be used in place of āmchur, and table or kosher salt may be used in place of black salt, both to taste. Seed the green chili when you first blend the chutney. You can always add seeds back in and blend again to make the chutney spicier if the first result lacks punch.

Date Chutney

MAKES ABOUT ½ CUP (150 G)

This sweet chutney is often served alongside green chutney (see page 212) with many Indian dishes, such as my Roasted Āloo Chāt, page 20. Date-tamarind chutney is another version; to make it, you can simply substitute 1 to 2 tablespoons tamarind paste or concentrate for the lemon juice.

PREP TIME 20 MINUTES

5 Medjool dates, pitted and roughly chopped (about ½ cup/75 g)

2 teaspoons fresh lime juice

¼ teaspoon cumin seeds

¼ teaspoon black salt

¼ teaspoon ground ginger

Pinch of ground red chili

Place all of the ingredients in a small saucepan with 1 cup (240 ml) water. Bring to a boil, then reduce the heat to a gentle simmer. Cook, uncovered, stirring occasionally until the dates resemble a paste, 10 to 15 minutes. Allow the mixture to cool slightly, then transfer to a blender. Blend, adding additional water 1 tablespoon at a time, until the desired consistency is reached (a thicker consistency is good for dipping, and thinner is good for chāt and drizzling). Adjust the seasoning to taste.

Chili Garlic Chutney

MAKES 2 TO 3 TABLESPOONS (ABOUT 25 G)

This chutney, when used cautiously, can elevate many a chāt (as on page 20) or shāk (vegetable dish; pages 66 to 87). It's one of my dad's favorites, and it's from Kāthiāwād, Gujarāt, the land of my paternal ancestors. This recipe uses a generous amount of garlic, which has been found to lower cholesterol levels,[30] making it beneficial against heart disease. Healthy or not, be warned: this chutney is pungent—a drop goes a long way! A user-friendly recipe, it can easily be scaled up or down and can be made from any combination of red chili that you prefer.

PREP TIME 10 MINUTES

1 garlic bulb, cloves peeled and roughly chopped

½ teaspoon salt, coarse if possible, or to taste

1 teaspoon ground mild red chili or paprika

½ teaspoon ground red chili, or to taste

Mash the garlic with the salt, which helps grind it, in a mortar until it forms a smooth paste, about 5 minutes (see Equipment Tip). Add the ground chili and mash well to combine. Add water, 1 teaspoon at a time, and stir until the desired consistency is reached. Refrigerate leftovers in an airtight container for about a month, if not longer.

EQUIPMENT TIP If you don't have a mortar and pestle, this recipe can be made in a blender. However, I wouldn't recommend it because the pungency of garlic and chili can linger in the blender container. The same thing can happen with a wooden mortar and pestle. Therefore, choose a ceramic or stone mortar and pestle, if possible.

Coconut Chutney

MAKES ABOUT 1¼ CUPS (300 G)

This is a popular South Indian chutney that's so delicious I could swim in it. I also like to serve it with Crispy Masālā Dosā Rolls (page 32). The peanuts give it a subtle nuttiness, but roasted chanā dāl (split black gram) is more traditional and can be used in its place.

PREP TIME 20 MINUTES

1⅓ cups (125 g) grated coconut, fresh or frozen and thawed

½ cup (120 ml) warm water, plus more as needed

¼ cup (36 g) unsalted roasted peanuts

½ green chili, seeded if desired

2 teaspoons minced ginger

2 teaspoons fresh lime juice (½ lime)

½ to ¾ teaspoon salt, or to taste

2 teaspoons neutral oil, such as avocado or sunflower

1 teaspoon split white urad dāl

1 teaspoon black mustard seeds

1 whole dried red chili, optional

Pinch of asafetida, optional

6 to 8 fresh curry leaves, torn

1 In a blender, combine the coconut, water, peanuts, green chili, ginger, lime juice, and salt. Blend until smooth, adding additional warm water 1 tablespoon at a time, if needed. Transfer to a serving bowl.

2 Heat the oil in a small saucepan over medium-high heat. Add the urad dāl and cook until just starting to brown, about 2 minutes, then add the mustard seeds. Continue to cook until the seeds begin to pop, about 30 seconds. Add the red chili and asafetida (if using), and swirl the pan for a few seconds. Remove from the heat, add the curry leaves, and cover. Swirl the pan so the leaves continue cooking in the remaining heat, about 1 minute.

3 Pour the seasoned oil mixture over the chutney in the serving bowl and stir well to combine. Add more water if a looser consistency is desired, adjust the seasoning to taste, and serve immediately.

STORAGE TIP Fresh is best, but leftovers may be stored in the refrigerator for up to 1 week. The chutney will thicken when refrigerated, so be sure to add more water and salt if needed when serving again.

Chhundo

MAKES ABOUT 1⅓ CUPS (360 G)

Chhundo is a sweet and sticky condiment (similar in texture to a marmalade) made from preserved green mango and warm spices. I gained appreciation for how it's traditionally made when I was on a summer trip in India. Shruti Foi, my paternal aunt, would fill a large steel pot with shredded mango, sugar, and spices and leave it out in the Mumbai sun all day. She'd bring it inside each night and repeat the process for about a week, or until the mixture had become a perfect, syrupy conserve. This version is a stovetop modification, since Chicagoland unfortunately has no such reliable sun, and it yields quite similar results. Beyond serving in its usual home as part of a thāli (platter) meal, this chhundo would be a lovely addition to a charcuterie board in place of marmalade. While traditional chhundo is stored in the pantry, I recommend storing this in the refrigerator. It will stay fresh for at least 1 week.

PREP TIME 45 MINUTES
COOK TIME 15 MINUTES

2 cups (about 275 g) peeled, seeded, and grated mango (1 large or 2 small mangoes, very green and firm to touch)

¾ cup (165 g) cane sugar (see Ingredient Tip)

½ teaspoon salt

1 teaspoon mild ground red chili or sweet paprika

¼ teaspoon freshly ground cardamom seeds (from about 4 pods)

¼ teaspoon cumin seeds, coarsely ground in a mortar

¼ teaspoon fennel seeds, coarsely ground in a mortar

¼ teaspoon ground cinnamon

⅛ teaspoon freshly ground cloves (about 4 cloves)

1 Mix the grated mango, sugar, and salt in a large bowl. Cover and let rest until the mango has released a significant amount of water, 20 to 30 minutes.

2 Transfer the mango and its liquid to a nonstick saucepan, stir in the red chili, cardamom, cumin, fennel, cinnamon, and cloves, and heat over medium-high heat until just simmering. Reduce the heat to maintain a simmer.

3 Simmer gently, stirring frequently, until thickened, about 10 minutes. The chhundo will thicken further as it cools, so don't cook it down too much. If it becomes too thick and crystallizes, add 1 to 2 tablespoons of water and reheat for 1 to 2 minutes.

4 Remove from the heat, transfer to a glass jar, and let the chhundo cool completely before enjoying.

INGREDIENT TIP I wouldn't recommend sugar substitutes for this recipe, as they will significantly alter the taste and texture of the final product.

Nondairy Yogurt

MAKES ABOUT 1¼ CUPS (300 G)

Yogurt, especially homemade yogurt, plays a large role in Indian cuisine. Creamy and tangy, yogurt pairs naturally with the warm spices of many Indian meals. The ritual of making yogurt is of utmost importance in Indian kitchens all over the world. Some families even have yogurt cultures dating back years, if not generations. Cashews are perfect for this plant-based version, which can be used in many other recipes, including Roasted Āloo Chāt (page 20), Nān (page 164), and Gujarāti Kadhi (page 121).

Store-bought nondairy yogurt is a great alternative if you prefer the convenience or need a base other than cashews due to dietary restriction or allergy. Be sure that it is unsweetened (or minimally sweetened) and plain before using it in or with the recipes in this book. I tasted more than ten brands for this book, and my favorites are Forager (cashew), Kite Hill (almond), Silk (soy), and So Delicious (coconut). The vegan yogurt market is ever evolving, so there will likely be even more (possibly better) choices available in the future.

PREP TIME 12 HOURS

1 cup (150 g) raw cashews
(see Ingredient Tip)

2 tablespoons unsweetened plain
nondairy yogurt

1 Soak the cashews in a large bowl filled with plenty of hot water (110 to 120°F/43 to 49°C) for 2 hours, then drain.

2 Blend the cashews with ¾ cup (180 ml) hot water. Transfer to a glass or steel container (with a tight-fitting lid) and gently stir in the yogurt until fully combined.

3 Cover with cheesecloth only (leaving the lid aside for now), and place in a warm spot (80 to 90°F/27 to 32°C) that gives protection from drafts (such as in the oven with the oven light on), for 12 hours (1 to 2 hours less for a less tangy product and 1 to 2 hours more for a tangier one). Cover the container with the lid and store in the refrigerator for up to 1 week.

INGREDIENT TIP Use raw cashews only for this recipe. Roasted cashews will work somewhat but will be nowhere near as good since they don't culture as well.

Mint Cucumber Rāitā

MAKES ABOUT 1¼ CUPS (250 G)

Rāitā is a cooling yogurt condiment that pairs particularly well with rich dishes, such as Mattar Tofu (page 90). This variation follows the most popular rāitā, which is made with cucumber. Adding mint makes it even more refreshing, and chāt masālā increases its tanginess.

PREP TIME 5 MINUTES

¾ cup (about 185 g) well-chilled, unsweetened plain nondairy yogurt (see page 223)

¼ to ½ English cucumber, chilled, seeded, and finely diced or grated

2 tablespoons finely chopped mint leaves

½ to 1 teaspoon chāt masālā (see page 236)

Stir all the ingredients together in a serving bowl until well combined. Serve immediately if cold, or store in the refrigerator to chill before serving.

VARIATION Add ½ avocado, finely diced, to this rāitā for an added layer of creamy richness.

Beet-Carrot Rāitā

MAKES ABOUT 1⅓ CUPS (300 G)

Rāitā comes in many forms, and this one is a less common but equally delicious variation. Carrots offer a pleasant sweetness, and the color from the beet will create a vibrant pop with any dish.

PREP TIME 10 MINUTES

¾ cup (about 185 g) unsweetened plain nondairy yogurt (see page 223)

½ small red or golden beet, peeled and finely grated

1 carrot, peeled if desired and finely grated

¼ teaspoon ground ginger

¼ teaspoon salt, plus more to taste

1 teaspoon neutral oil, such as avocado or sunflower

½ teaspoon black mustard seeds

Pinch of asafetida, optional

6 to 8 curry leaves

1 Whisk together the yogurt, beet, carrot, ginger, and salt in a medium bowl.

2 Heat the oil in a small saucepan over medium-high heat until glossy, 30 seconds. Add the mustard seeds and asafetida (if using), and heat until the seeds crackle, about 1 minute.

3 Remove from the heat and add the curry leaves. Cover immediately and swirl the saucepan around until the leaves begin to crisp, about 30 seconds. Pour the seasoned oil over the rāitā, stir well, and serve immediately.

Garam Masālā Dressing

MAKES ABOUT ¾ CUP (175 G)

This creamy dressing, warmed by the spices in garam masālā, is key to Garam Masālā and Pāpad Salad (page 63). It can also be used in wraps or sandwiches in place of mayo.

PREP TIME 5 MINUTES

¼ cup (35 g) unsalted cashews, raw or roasted, soaked in hot water for 15 minutes and drained

2 tablespoons fresh lemon juice (1 lemon)

2 tablespoons extra virgin olive oil

1 tablespoon maple syrup or desired sweetener, or to taste

1½ teaspoons Dijon mustard

1½ teaspoons garam masālā (see page 232)

¾ teaspoon salt, or to taste

Combine all of the ingredients in a blender. Blend until very smooth, adding 1 to 2 tablespoons water to reach the preferred consistency. Adjust the seasoning to taste. Serve immediately or store in the refrigerator for up to 1 week.

VARIATION For a nut-free alternative, use sunflower seeds or hemp hearts instead of cashews.

MASĀLĀ

Spice Blends

Store-bought spice blends from Indian grocery stores are a completely reasonable option (I use them, too), but mastery of the four spice blends in this chapter will take your cooking to a new level. Spices can take your health to a new level, too! Turmeric and cardamom have powerful anti-inflammatory properties. Cumin has even been shown to play a role in weight loss as well.[31]

Making these spice blends at home from whole spices will ensure a freshness that surpasses any store-bought variety. They appear in the recipes throughout this book, and you'll find that they are the building blocks for numerous other spice blends you can make to suit your own tastes. I recommend using a spice grinder (or a coffee grinder used only for spices) for the best results. These spice blends can also be made with a mortar and pestle, but it will take much more time and effort. Store the ground spices in an airtight container for up to 3 months, but since the recipes make smaller batches, you can use them up quickly to ensure their freshness.

Garam Masālā

MAKES ½ CUP (ABOUT 56 G)

Garam masālā means "warm spice blend" in Hindi, and it provides incredible nuance and warmth without spicy heat. It is used widely throughout North Indian cuisine and in the recipes in this book. Black cardamom (which offers smoky depth) and mace (the outer coating of nutmeg, which lends a subtle floral sweetness) may be more difficult to find at your average grocer, but I recommend sourcing them from an Indian grocer or online. Feel free to omit them if they're not available.

PREP TIME 15 MINUTES

¼ cup (17 g) coriander seeds

2 tablespoons cumin seeds

1½ tablespoons fennel seeds

24 green cardamom pods, husks removed (about 1 teaspoon seeds)

2 bay leaves, torn, optional

2 black cardamom pods, husks removed (about ½ teaspoon seeds), optional

1 cinnamon stick (3 inches/7.5 cm)

1 star anise

½ nutmeg, crushed

1 small piece mace, optional

1 teaspoon cloves (about 20)

½ teaspoon black peppercorns (about 25)

1 Heat a pan over medium-low heat and toast the coriander, cumin, and fennel seeds until lightly browned and fragrant, 3 to 5 minutes. Transfer to a bowl to cool.

2 Add the green cardamom, bay leaves (if using), black cardamom (if using), cinnamon, star anise, nutmeg, mace (if using), cloves, and peppercorns to the pan and toast until fragrant, 3 to 5 minutes. Transfer to the bowl with the other toasted seeds. Allow the spices to cool completely, then blend to a powder in a spice grinder. Store in an airtight container for up to 3 months.

Sāmbār Podi

MAKES ½ CUP (ABOUT 56 G)

Podi is the name for ground spices that's used in several South Indian languages (including Tamil and Telugu). This blend is for use with Sāmbār (page 114). Most versions of podi include red chilies, but I prefer to leave them out and add ground red chili during cooking instead. This allows me to adjust the spiciness of any dish without sacrificing the core characteristics of this spice blend, which are warm, toasty, nutty, and subtly bitter.

PREP TIME 15 MINUTES

1 tablespoon chanā dāl
  (split Bengal gram)

1 tablespoon split white urad dāl

¼ cup (16 g) coriander seeds

1 tablespoon cumin seeds

½ teaspoon fenugreek seeds

½ teaspoon black peppercorns

20 fresh curry leaves

1 teaspoon ground turmeric

1 Place the chanā and urad dāls in a medium pan over medium heat. Toast dry in the pan, stirring frequently, until lightly browned, about 5 minutes. Transfer to a bowl.

2 Reduce the heat to medium-low, add the coriander seeds, cumin seeds, fenugreek seeds, and peppercorns to the pan and toast, stirring frequently, until lightly browned and fragrant, about 5 minutes. Transfer to the bowl with the dāl.

3 Toast the fresh curry leaves in the pan until dry and crisp, about 3 minutes, then transfer them to the same bowl. Let all of the spices cool completely, then blend into a powder in a spice grinder. Stir in the ground turmeric, then store in an airtight container for up to 3 months.

Chāt Masālā

MAKES ABOUT ⅓ CUP (40 G)

This tangy, pungent, irresistible spice blend is used in many street food dishes, including chāt (see page 20). Store-bought chāt masālā is fine to use, but here's a recipe for making a fresher version at home.

PREP TIME 10 MINUTES

2 tablespoons cumin seeds

1 tablespoon coriander seeds

1 tablespoon fennel seeds

½ teaspoon black peppercorns

2 teaspoons black salt (kālā namak)

1½ teaspoons āmchur (dried green mango powder)

½ teaspoon ground ginger

¼ teaspoon asafetida, optional

Toast the cumin seeds, coriander seeds, fennel seeds, and peppercorns in a medium pan over medium-low heat until lightly browned and fragrant, about 5 minutes. Remove the spices from the pan, let cool, then blend to a powder in a spice grinder. Combine with the black salt, āmchur, ginger, and asafetida (if using). Store in an airtight container for up to 3 months.

Chāi Masālā

This fragrant and subtle spice blend, intended for sweet applications, can be used to make Masālā Chāi (page 197) or to add chāi flavor to desserts (e.g., Chocolate Chāi Mousse with Berries, page 178). Beyond the flavor, the spice combination is also a nutritional powerhouse. Black pepper and cardamom have roles in maintaining our immune system and even in cancer prevention![32]

PREP TIME 15 MINUTES

40 green cardamom pods, husks removed (about 1½ teaspoons seeds)

10 cloves

2 teaspoons fennel seeds

1 star anise, optional

½ teaspoon black peppercorns

1 cinnamon stick (3 inches/7.5 cm), broken into pieces

1 teaspoon ground ginger

½ small nutmeg, freshly grated (about 1 teaspoon)

Place the cardamom, cloves, fennel seeds, star anise (if using), and peppercorns in a spice grinder. Blend to a fine powder, transfer to a bowl, add the cinnamon, ginger, and nutmeg, and put in a small airtight container. Store in the pantry for up to 3 months.

Tomato Onion Masālā

MAKES 1½ CUPS (375 G)

This masālā and the Smoky Tomato Onion Masālā (page 242) form the basis for the gravy-based dishes in this book. This recipe does require some effort, but it can easily be made in advance. It also freezes well (up to 6 months), so don't hesitate to make larger batches. Simply defrost in the refrigerator overnight, then use in your desired gravy dish (see pages 88 to 105).

PREP TIME 10 MINUTES
COOK TIME 45 MINUTES

2 teaspoons olive oil

1 yellow onion, diced
(about 2 cups/300 g)

½ teaspoon salt, plus more to taste

6 garlic cloves, minced or crushed
(about 1½ tablespoons)

1½ tablespoons minced ginger

1 teaspoon garam masālā
(see page 232)

1 teaspoon ground coriander

1 teaspoon ground cumin

½ teaspoon ground red chili

½ teaspoon ground turmeric

⅓ cup (90 g) tomato paste

1 Heat the oil in a wide pan or braising pan over medium heat. Add the onion and salt, and cook, stirring occasionally, until softened and starting to brown, about 15 minutes. Adjust the heat between medium-low and medium to prevent the onions from browning too quickly.

2 Reduce the heat to medium-low. Add the garlic and ginger and continue to stir until lightly browned and fragrant, 3 to 5 minutes.

3 Add the garam masālā, coriander, cumin, red chili, and turmeric, and stir for a few seconds to toast. Add the tomato paste and 1 cup (240 ml) water and stir well to combine. Increase the heat to medium and cook, stirring occasionally, until thickened, about 10 minutes.

4 Transfer the onion and tomato mixture to a blender, let it cool slightly, and blend until smooth. Store in an airtight container and refrigerate for a few days or freeze for up to 6 months.

Smoky Tomato Onion Masālā

MAKES 2 CUPS (500 G)

This variation on the Tomato Onion Masālā (page 240) gets its smokiness and additional depth of flavor from black cardamom, fire-roasted tomatoes, and smoked paprika. I use this masālā as the basis for Rājmā (page 97).

PREP TIME 10 MINUTES
COOK TIME 45 MINUTES

2 teaspoons olive oil

1 bay leaf

1 black cardamom pod, optional but recommended

1 yellow onion, diced (about 2 cups/300 g)

½ teaspoon salt, plus more to taste

8 garlic cloves, minced (about 2 tablespoons)

1 tablespoon minced ginger

1 teaspoon garam masālā (see page 232)

1 teaspoon ground coriander

1 teaspoon ground cumin

½ teaspoon ground red chili, or to taste

½ teaspoon ground turmeric

½ teaspoon smoked paprika

One 14.5-ounce (410 g) can crushed tomatoes (fire-roasted, if possible)

1   Heat the oil in a wide pan or braising pan over medium heat. Add the bay leaf, cardamom (if using), onion, and salt, and cook, stirring occasionally, until onion is softened and starting to brown, about 15 minutes.

2   Lower the heat to medium-low, add the garlic and ginger, and continue to stir until fragrant, 3 to 5 minutes.

3   Add the garam masālā, coriander, cumin, red chili, turmeric, and paprika, stir to lightly toast, about 30 seconds, then stir in the crushed tomatoes.

4   Increase the heat to medium and cook, stirring occasionally, until the tomatoes are reduced and jammy, about 15 minutes.

5   Transfer the onion and tomato mixture to a blender, let it cool slightly, and blend until smooth. Store in an airtight container and refrigerate for a few days or freeze for up to 6 months.

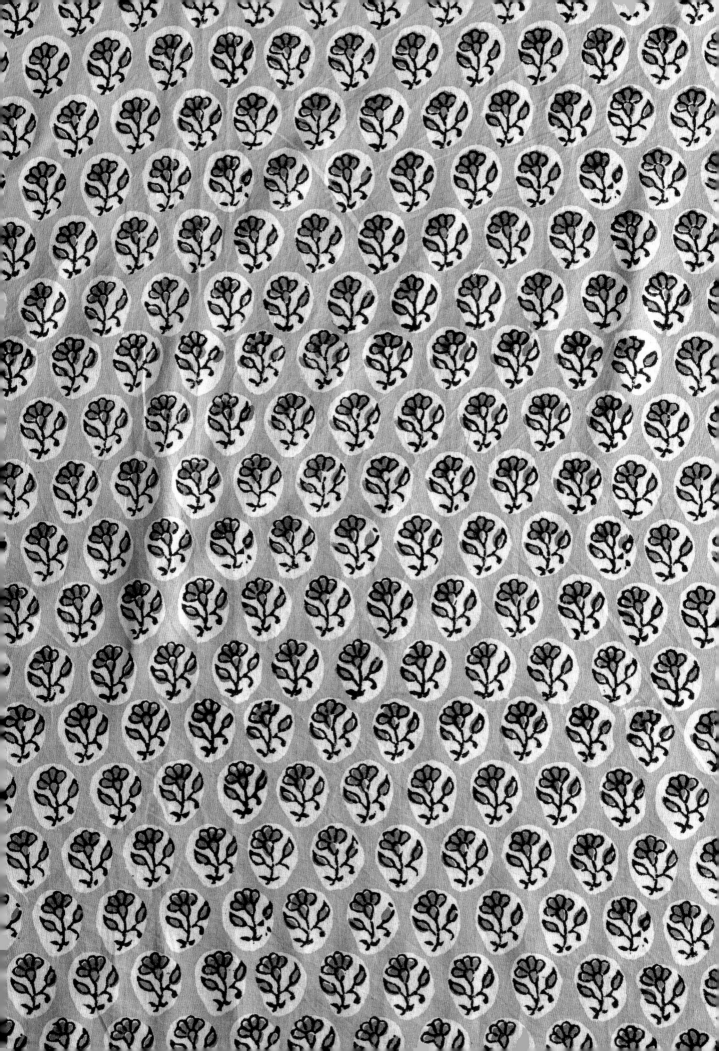

NOTES

1 Angelino, D., et al., "Fruit and Vegetable Consumption and Health Outcomes: An Umbrella Review of Observational Studies," *International Journal of Food Sciences and Nutrition* 70, no. 6 (2019): 652–67.

2 Lidder, S., et al., "Vascular Effects of Dietary Nitrate (as Found in Green Leafy Vegetables and Beetroot) via the Nitrate-Nitrite-Nitric Oxide Pathway," *British Journal of Clinical Pharmacology* 75, no. 3 (2013): 677–96.

3 Parks, K., et al., "Culinary Medicine: Paving the Way to Health Through Our Forks," *American Journal of Lifestyle Medicine* 14, no. 1 (2019): 51–53.

4 Devries, S., et al., "Nutrition Education in Medical School, Residency Training, and Practice," *JAMA* 321, no. 14 (2019): 1351.

5 "Guidelines & Clinical Documents," American College of Cardiology, acc.org.

6 "Clinical Practice Guidelines and Recommendations," American College of Physicians, acponline.org.

7 American College of Lifestyle Medicine, lifestylemedicine.org.

8 Bazzano, L. A., et al., "Legume Consumption and Risk of Coronary Heart Disease in US Men and Women: NHANES I Epidemiologic Follow-Up Study," *ACC Current Journal Review* 11, no. 2 (2002): 31–32.

9 Li, H., et al., "Legume Consumption and All-Cause and Cardiovascular Disease Mortality," *BioMed Research International* (2017): 1–6.

10 Ma, L., et al., "Isoflavone Intake and the Risk of Coronary Heart Disease in US Men and Women," *Circulation* 141, no. 14 (2020): 1127–37.

11 Park, W., et al., "New Perspectives of Curcumin in Cancer Prevention," *Cancer Prevention Research* 6, no. 5 (2013): 387–400.

12 "American Cancer Society Guideline for Diet and Physical Activity," American Cancer Society, cancer.org/healthy/eat-healthy-get-active/acs-guidelines-nutrition-physical-activity-cancer-prevention/guidelines.html. Accessed August 9, 2021.

13 Melina, V., et al., "Position of the Academy of Nutrition and Dietetics: Vegetarian Diets," *Journal of the Academy of Nutrition and Dietetics* 116, no. 12 (2016): 1970–80.

14 Joshi, S., et al., "Plant-Based Diets and Hypertension," *American Journal of Lifestyle Medicine* 14, no. 4 (2020): 397–405.

15 Barnard, N. D., et al., "A Low-Fat Vegan Diet Improves Glycemic Control and Cardiovascular Risk Factors in a Randomized Clinical Trial in Individuals with Type 2 Diabetes," *Diabetes Care* 29, no. 8 (2006): 1777–83.

16 "Physical Activity Guidelines for Americans," US Department of Health and Human Services, Office of Disease Prevention and Health Promotion, health.gov/sites/default/files/2019-10/PAG_ExecutiveSummary.pdf. Accessed August 9, 2021.

17 Chida, Y., et al., "Positive Psychological Well-Being and Mortality: A Quantitative Review of Prospective Observational Studies," *Psychosomatic Medicine* 70, no. 7 (2008): 741–56.

18 Aggarwal, B. B., et al., "Curcumin: The Indian Solid Gold," *Advances in Experimental Medicine and Biology* 595 (2007): 1–75.

19 Breithaupt-Grögler, K., et al., "Protective Effect of Chronic Garlic Intake on Elastic Properties of Aorta in the Elderly," *Circulation* 96, no. 8 (1997): 2649–55.

20 Lee, H. Y., et al., "1-Dehydro-[10]-gingerdione from Ginger Inhibits Ikkβ Activity for NF-κB Activation and Suppresses NF-κB-Regulated Expression of Inflammatory Genes," *British Journal of Pharmacology* 167, no. 1 (2012): 128–40.

21 Jacobs, A., "Is Dairy Farming Cruel to Cows?," *The New York Times*, December 29, 2020.

22 "Protecting Farm Animals," American Society for the Prevention of Cruelty to Animals (ASPCA), aspca.org/protecting-farm-animals.

23 "5 Myths about the Dairy Industry," The Humane League, thehumaneleague.org/article/dairy-industry-myths.

24 Bekoff, M., "Is Dairy Farming Cruel to Bright and Emotional Cows?," *Psychology Today*, January 7, 2021.

25 Jacobson, M. S., "Cholesterol Oxides in Indian Ghee: Possible Cause of Unexplained High Risk of Atherosclerosis in Indian Immigrant Populations," *The Lancet* 330, no. 8560 (1987): 656–58.

26 Fernando, W., et al., "Diets Supplemented with Chickpea or Its Main Oligosaccharide Component Raffinose Modify Faecal Microbial Composition in Healthy Adults," *Beneficial Microbes* 1, no. 2 (2010): 197–207.

27 Davis, P. A., et al., "Cinnamon Intake Lowers Fasting Blood Glucose: Meta-Analysis," *Journal of Medicinal Food* 14, no. 9 (2011): 884–89.

28 Bhattacharjee, B., et al., "Identification of Proapoptopic, Anti-Inflammatory, Anti-Proliferative, Anti-Invasive and Anti-Angiogenic Targets of Essential Oils in Cardamom by Dual Reverse Virtual Screening and Binding Pose Analysis," *Asian Pacific Journal of Cancer Prevention* 14, no. 6 (2013): 3735–42.

29 Tebb, Z. D., "Dark Chocolate Improves Coronary Vasomotion and Reduces Platelet Reactivity," *The Journal of Emergency Medicine* 34, no. 4 (2008): 494.

30 Ried, K., et al., "Effect of Garlic on Serum Lipids: An Updated Meta-Analysis," *Nutrition Reviews* 71, no. 5 (2013): 282–99.

31 Taghizadeh, M., et al., "Effect of the *Cumin Cyminum* L. Intake on Weight Loss, Metabolic Profiles and Biomarkers of Oxidative Stress in Overweight Subjects: A Randomized Double-Blind Placebo-Controlled Clinical Trial," *Annals of Nutrition and Metabolism* 66, no. 2–3 (2015): 117–24.

32 Majdalawieh, A. F., et al., "In Vitro Investigation of the Potential Immunomodulatory and Anti-Cancer Activities of Black Pepper (*Piper nigrum*) and Cardamom (*Elettaria cardamomum*)," *Journal of Medicinal Food* 13, no. 2 (2010): 371–81.

ACKNOWLEDGMENTS

Shrey, my son, thank you for being my shining light and number one motivator. Thank you for giving me the greatest gift of fatherhood and for allowing me to learn and grow with you. I look forward to cooking these recipes with you for many years to come!

Rachel, my wife, thank you for championing this project before I even dreamed it up. Thank you for being my love, life partner, most critical editor, master recipe tester, patient hand model, rās partner, dāl to my bhāt, and so much more.

Dr. Sanjeev and Sonal Shukla, my parents, thank you for always supporting my every endeavor with excitement and eagerness. Thank you for being the foodies you are and for also allowing me to enjoy all that life has to offer from a young age.

Dr. Shawn Shukla and Dr. Roaya Namdari, my brother and sister-in-law, thank you for being my role models and best friends. Thank you for teaching me about kindness and humility through example.

Pradip and Daxa Tailor, my parents-in-law, thank you for introducing me to your own family cuisines and traditions and for enriching the recipes in this book that much further. Thank you also for all your behind-the-scenes efforts in making this book a reality.

Charlie Brotherstone, my literary agent, thank you for navigating me through the world of publishing and for connecting me with the most incredible publishing team.

Olivia Peluso, editor extraordinaire, thank you for believing in this project from the very beginning and for celebrating every aspect of my vision. Thank you for being so cognizant of the nuances of Indian culture and for allowing my personal heritage to shine.

The amazing team at The Experiment—especially Matthew Lore, Peter Burri, Jennifer Hergenroeder, Beth Bugler, Melinda Kennedy, Zach Pace, Pamela Schechter, Margie Guerra, Will Rhino, Irmak Donahue, and Valerie Saint-Rossy—thank you for your incredible attention to detail in every aspect of the creation of this book and for bringing this book to life.

Soula Pefkaros (Golden Ratio Clay Works), thank you for creating the stunning ceramic thāli featured on the cover and throughout this book. Dubhe Carreño (This Quiet Dust Ceramics), thank you for sharing your work with me and allowing me to showcase it in the book's photography. Thank you also to the ceramic artists of East Fork Pottery and Gaya Ceramic, Danielle Chutinthranond (Monsoon Pottery), Bina (Mud Bloom Pottery), and Cara Janelle, whose wonderful work made photographing the recipes that much more enjoyable.

My extended family, friends, Instagram community, and residency mentors and colleagues: This book would not be a reality without your support and well wishes. I'm forever grateful.

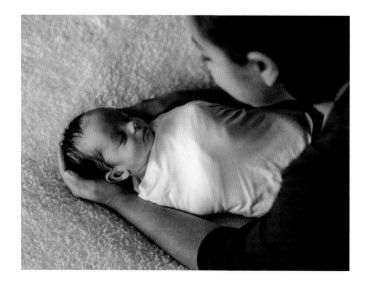

RECIPE TESTERS AND THEIR FAVORITE RECIPES

A huge thank-you to everyone who tested the recipes in this book: Anusha (Yummy Yatra), Bhavika Tailor, Chaitanya Rani, Danielle Ornelas, Dhara Puvar, Dharati Desai & Vatsal Doshi, Florine Knotnerus, Heather Sin, Heran Bhakta, Janki Patel, Jessi Jordan, Jessica Babine, Jessica Soul, Kshama P, Lesley Atlansky, Manjari V. Kansal, Meghna Murali, Monika Sharda, Nina R, Prachi Shah, Preeti Sidhu, Puja Bhagwakar, Radha & Raffi, Ravina Gandhakwala & Miraj Chokshi, Roshni & Parth Patel, Chef Ruchi Coelho, Ruchita Doshi, Rupal Sachdev, Sampoorna Biswas, Sarah Kossler, Shivani K. Patel, Sima Desai, Snehal, Tracy Harris Levene, Vandan Koria, Vrushti Buch.

Here's what my incredible testers had to say about some of the recipes:

Roasted Āloo Chāt: "This was my favorite of all the recipes I tested! I would have been more than happy eating the roasted potatoes on their own, but turning them into chāt was beyond delicious. I love the balance of savory and sweet chutneys and the creamy and crunchy textures." **—Nina**

Creamy Chili Pasta: "Honestly, my reaction was 'wow!' The whole family raved about it. The sauce was so flavorful! When I told my mother-in-law what was in it, she couldn't believe it was so healthy and exclaimed about how silky it was. The sauce was a great consistency, and it disguised the fact that they were eating whole wheat pasta. Totally a winner. Would definitely make again." **—Lesley**

Garam Masālā and Pāpad Salad: "LOVED IT . . . would make it again and again." **—Radha & Raffi**

Chhole: "Pleasingly complex, rich, great balance of spices. My new favorite way to make this dish." **—Nina**

Dāl Makhani: "Wow. I took one bite of this just as it ended cooking, how delicious!! I was just so shocked I made something that tasted so good." **—Jessica B.**

Gujarāti Dāl: "I was so surprised how much I enjoyed making and eating this dāl given that I was never a fan of Gujarāti dāl growing up. It made me miss my mom and prompted me to call her—would say that was my favorite, along with the fact that it was easy to make and it tasted great when I followed all the measurements for spices." **—Dharati & Vatsal**

Vegetable Khichadi: "Flavorful, hearty, and comforting. Khichadi is not always my favorite dish, but the depth of flavor and variety of textures made this one excellent. The suggested lime juice and cilantro were great for adding brightness as well. I loved how vegetable-packed and adaptable this recipe is. I also liked that the leftovers kept and reheated well—the flavors only got better!" **—Nina**

Cilantro Peanut Chutney: "Delicious! This was one of the best chutneys I have ever had! The best part of this chutney is how you've substituted sugar with a date. I think it's a brilliant idea and it makes this chutney so delicious and naturally sweetened. The chutney is just perfect in terms of color, flavor, consistency, and spice. I liked this chutney so much that I ended up eating a bowl of it on its own and licked the jar off!" **—Vrushti**

Masālā Chāi: "This is a perfectly balanced chāi. Really wonderful! Spice very present but not too aggressive. Sugar is also perfect, not too sweet." **–Tracy**

Chocolate Chāi Mousse with Berries: "This recipe is going to be an absolute winner! I've had tofu mousse before, but this is next level. It was light but felt decadent. The chāi masālā was balanced and flavor forward and tasted great in our evening chāi. It was such a great addition to the mousse." **–Manjari**

RESOURCES

ONLINE

Sheil Shukla, (author website; sheilshukla.com)

Nutrition Facts, Dr. Michael Greger (nutritionfacts.org)

Physicians Committee for Responsible Medicine (pcrm.org)

Plant-Based Eating Guide, Kaiser Permanente (kphealthyme.com/ documents/plant_based_ diet_e.aspx)

Forks over Knives (forksoverknives.com)

BOOKS

The 30-Day Alzheimer's Solution, by Dean Sherzai, MD, and Ayesha Sherzai, MD

72 Reasons to Be Vegan, by Gene Stone and Kathy Freston

Fiber Fueled, by Will Bulsiewicz, MD

Forks over Knives, edited by Gene Stone

How Not to Die, by Michael G. Greger, MD, and Gene Stone

Main Street Vegan, by Victoria Moran and Adair Moran

Nourish, by Reshma Shah, MD, and Brenda Davis

Plant-Proof, by Simon Hill

Prevent and Reverse Heart Disease, by Caldwell B. Esselstyn Jr., MD

Vegan Intermittent Fasting, by Petra Bracht, MD, and Mira Flatt

Whole: Rethinking the Science of Nutrition, by T. Colin Campbell, PhD, and Howard Jacobson, PhD

DOCUMENTARY FILMS

Cowspiracy (2014)

Forks over Knives (2011)

The Game Changers (2018)

Seaspiracy (2021)

Vegucated (2011)

What the Health (2017)

INDEX

ABOUT THE AUTHOR

Sheil Shukla, DO, is an internal medicine physician and food artist who is passionate about the intersection of food, art, and medicine. He loves exploring cultures through their food, and his primary experience is with South Asian foods. His culinary creations have garnered the support of over 58,000 followers on Instagram. He is also a contributor for Best of Vegan, a digital culinary publication dedicated to veganism and plant-based cuisine, and he has been featured by VegNews, THRIVE Magazine, the FeedFeed, Food52, Williams-Sonoma, and more.

As a Doctor of Osteopathic Medicine (DO), Sheil Shukla has studied and rigorously trained in medicine with an emphasis on treating the whole person. He takes a holistic approach with a focus on prevention as opposed to solely symptom management. He earned his doctorate at the Chicago College of Osteopathic Medicine at Midwestern University, and he completed his residency training in internal medicine at Lutheran General Hospital in Park Ridge, Illinois. He has also earned a certificate in plant-based nutrition through the T. Colin Campbell Center for Nutrition Studies at Cornell University. While he was writing this book, Sheil Shukla was also preparing for board certification exams in internal medicine and eventually lifestyle medicine.

Sheil Shukla lives in Chicagoland with his wife, Rachel, and son, Shrey.

sheilshukla.com | ⓘ plantbasedartist